Wait No More captures the beauty of we are all made in God's image, created for a purpose, one family. As the Rosatis tell their personal story of the Lord-led journey to fulfill the family He intended for them, you cannot help but come away with the certainty that God truly works all things together for the good when we follow His plan for our lives. It won't always be easy, but it is certainly worth it. This is a great read for anyone who is considering adoption or needs a word of encouragement and assurance that God is in control.

> —WILLIAM J. BLACQUIERE
> President & CEO, Bethany Christian Services

This is a book that will grip you from the inside out and not let go until you have caught the heart of God for the orphans among us. Sharing candid details of their own journey, Kelly and John Rosati's story will help all of us count the cost before saying yes to the adventure and miracle of adoption.

> —BRADY BOYD
> Senior Pastor, New Life Church
> Author, *Fear No Evil*
> Dad to two adopted children, Abram and Callie

Kelly and John Rosati have written an honest look at foster care adoption and all the challenges and emotions that come with that journey. The way that God has held and directed this family through the adoption process is an inspiration to others who find themselves journeying the same unpredictable path. An honest telling of the joys that come through while fighting for the family that God designed them to have, this story will encourage believers and the church to mobilize and move tenaciously to help the world's 140 million plus children who find themselves orphaned.

—MARY BETH CHAPMAN
President, Show Hope
New York Times Best-Selling Author, *Choosing to SEE*

Our friends Kelly and John have big hearts—hearts that ache for kids who are often overlooked by society. The miracle of adoption has turned their world upside down. Has it been an easy process? No, but as the Rosatis will tell you, good things are worth fighting for.

—JIM AND JEAN DALY
Jim is president of Focus on the Family
and author of *Finding Home* and *Stronger*

Our world is in need of something more than a good story; it needs a God story. *Wait No More* is about the kind of life every family dreams to live—risky and uncertain but filled with a faith that is vibrant and alive in a God who is with them every step of the way. Reading this book will inspire you to live for things bigger than this world can imagine.

—TOM DAVIS
CEO, Children's HopeChest
Author, *Fields of the Fatherless* and *Priceless*

Usually when I read a book I read the first two chapters, the end, and then the two middle chapters, and I'm done. I couldn't do that with this book. The power of this message will make the difference in the lives of children/youth, families, and churches around this nation. The Rosatis' journey of building their family through adoption from the foster care system became my journey. I read and wept. And I read and cheered. And then I read Chapter 24 and just sobbed and thanked God. Every child/youth in foster care waits for a family that will care, nurture, advocate, and fight to keep them safe and meet their needs. These four children wait no more. The Rosatis' intercession for other children brings hope that others will be inspired to adopt from foster care. Because every child/youth deserves to grow up in a family.

—SHAREN FORD, PH.D.

Manager, Permanency Services, Colorado
Department of Human Services

Adoption mirrors the gospel story, not only in its joy but often in great sacrifices as well. Adoption draws us closer to the world's hurt, even as it reminds us of the preciousness of every child and the sweetness when love springs up where only pain had lived before. *Wait No More* carries all of this, showing one family's experience of how beauty and sorrow so often intertwine in an adoption journey. Sometimes raw, sometimes joyous, always honest, *Wait No More* will undoubtedly spur many families to question whether adoption may be too difficult a road for them . . . and also whether any other path could bring such great rewards.

—JEDD MEDEFIND

President, Christian Alliance for Orphans

In *Wait No More*, we are given a very intimate and transparent look into how the Lord transforms lives and a family through adoption. Kelly and John demonstrate that the only reason to adopt a child is to love him or her unconditionally. By being available for how God wanted to use them, the Rosatis paint for the reader a very real picture of how adoption is a journey in which we often join in the sufferings of Christ, but in so doing, experience amazing joy as well.

—PAUL PENNINGTON
Executive Director & Co-Founder, Hope for Orphans

In *Wait No More,* Kelly Rosati contextualizes a personal narrative that reconciles a pro-life conviction with the compassionate action of adoption. Kelly demonstrates that in the 21st century, prophetic witness must accompany Christian outreach even in the most dire of circumstances. This book captures the heart of the gospel message as this generation reaches out to the orphan and the hurting, all in the name of Christ.

—REVEREND SAMUEL RODRIGUEZ
President, National Hispanic Christian
Leadership Conference (NHCLC)

Wait No More is a touching story of Kelly and John Rosati's personal journey of faith and obedience, leading them to the adoption of four very needy children. As believers in Christ, we have been given a biblical mandate to "care for the least of these," without excuse. And clearly, children without a loving home are the neediest of all. *Wait No More* will open your eyes to the growing numbers and plight of orphans in our world today. The stories in this book will break your heart and challenge you to action.

—DR. WESS STAFFORD
President & CEO, Compassion International

Wait No More

Kelly & John Rosati

Tyndale House Publishers, Inc.
Carol Stream, Illinois

A Focus on the Family book published by
Tyndale House Publishers, Inc., Carol Stream, Illinois 60188

Focus on the Family and the accompanying logo and design are federally registered trademarks of Focus on the Family, Colorado Springs, CO 80995.

TYNDALE and Tyndale's quill logo are registered trademarks of Tyndale House Publishers, Inc.

Editor: Brandy Bruce
Cover photograph taken by Stephen Vosloo. Copyright © by Focus on the Family. All rights reserved.
Cover design by Jacqueline L. Nuñez
Photos of Hope and Joshua (top and right) on page 7 of insert and family photo on page 8 of insert taken by Stephen Vosloo. Copyright © by Focus on the Family. All rights reserved.

People's names and certain details of their stories have been changed to protect the privacy of the individuals involved. However, the facts of what happened and the underlying principles have been conveyed as accurately as possible.

The use of material from or references to various websites does not imply endorsement of those sites in their entirety.

Library of Congress Cataloging-in-Publication Data
Rosati, Kelly, 1968-
  Wait no more : one family's amazing adoption journey / by Kelly and John Rosati.
     p. cm.
  ISBN 978-1-58997-653-5
1. Adoption--Religious aspects--Christianity. I. Rosati, John. II. Title.
  HV875.26.R67 2011
  362.734092--dc23

                          2011020912

Printed in the United States of America

1 2 3 4 5 6 7 8 9 / 16 15 14 13 12 11

*This book is dedicated to our heavenly Father, who adopted us
through faith in Jesus Christ. Without His love, we are nothing.
And to our precious four kiddos, who have enriched
our lives immeasurably. You are gifts from God.
May our family be a testimony of God's unconditional love and grace.
And to all the children still waiting for their forever families.
May they wait no more.*

———

Contents

Acknowledgments

Who could have imagined that writing an Acknowledgments page would be one of the most daunting aspects of writing a book? John and I are loath to forget any of those to whom we owe great thanks. If you find yourself being one of those people, please forgive us in advance. Our list of people to thank could go on for pages! Instead, we're keeping it brief. Many others who have offered us support and encouragement along the way are mentioned in the book itself.

To DeeannaMarie and Randy Wallace—how can we adequately thank you? God used your faithful witness and encouragement to start us on this incredible journey.

We are grateful to our parents for all their love and support and to our siblings and their families—we love you all. And we love how you've always loved our children. To all our family members in the East Coast, Midwest, Rocky Mountains, and Hawaii—thank you.

Mahalo nui loa (thank you very much) to Pastor Ron, to "Uncle Pastor" Chris, and to our beloved church family at Kaimuki Christian Church. You were such a huge blessing to us throughout our journey. We love and miss you very much.

To all our friends who supported us through our Colorado trials—thank you. You are friends who truly carry one another's burdens.

We owe great thanks to the best editor ever, Brandy Bruce. Thank you for your patience and skill with these novice writers. Thank you to Larry Weeden for suggesting and believing in this project.

To Jim Daly for his heart for orphans that enabled the Wait No More program. Children have families because of your commitment.

Thanks, too, to the Adoption & Orphan Care team at Focus on the Family. Katie and Erin, you're the best. It's an honor to work with you!

Special thanks to all of you for taking the time to read this book. We pray God will use it to bless your lives.

And most of all, thanks to God. May we ever live to know Your love and make You known.

A Picture
of Our Future

I felt as if I was losing my mind. In one quick swoop, my belief
that I was following God's will for my life, that my husband,
John, and I were going in the right direction, was replaced by
doubt, fear, frustration, and anger. I cried out to God for help.

What had started out as a deep desire to help a child in need
had left John and me spiraling into despair. Surely this wasn't God's
plan for us. Or was it? All I knew was that something had gone terribly wrong. And that my passionate hope to make a difference had
turned our lives upside down. If someone had told this Midwestern
girl just a few years before that I would be living in Hawaii, serving
as a foster mother to an eleven-year-old girl, and feeling completely
ready to pull out my hair, I wouldn't have believed it.

Our friend Deeanna had taken Angie, the eleven-year-old girl
who was living with us, away for the weekend. John and I needed
a break. We needed to regroup. During those few days, John and I
wrestled mightily with the Lord about whether we could keep Angie

in our home. We'd known it was only supposed to be a temporary arrangement. But after just one month, we were ready to quit.

Can you believe it? Only one month, and we were in hell.

I kept wondering how I'd gotten to this place in my life.

———⊗⊗⊗———

It was April 16, 2000. John and I were living in Hawaii—John's third air force assignment—and I was working as the executive director for the Hawaii Family Forum (HFF), a nonprofit organization that provided pro-family education to local churches and the community. John and I had been happily married for eight years. The truth was that we'd always planned to have a family but wanted to wait until John's military assignments were more stable. The last thing we ever wanted was to be separated or to have children constantly moving around. We were also committed to my being home with our children when they were babies, and we simply weren't in a financial position yet for that to happen.

We loved our lives and enjoyed our time together immensely. But by the time we decided we were ready to have children, nothing happened. And yet interestingly, and somewhat unusually, we weren't fazed by it. For several months we tried to get pregnant, but the months came and went with no change. It just wasn't happening. We experienced some disappointment each month, but not overwhelming disappointment or grief.

John and I both have said that sometimes it seems easier to trust God in the really big things than it does in the small things, and this was one of those big things that was out of our control. God's timing was also significant. From the rearview mirror, it's clear to us now that God just swept us right into the next phase of life.

We always believed that if we weren't getting pregnant, there was a reason. And to us, adoption seemed like the obvious reason, though we weren't ready to pursue it right then. We know it's not how others might have felt in the same situation, and believe me, the ease with which we stepped through that period of life had nothing to do with us. We attribute it to God's grace. Nothing more. We figured God had a different plan for us down the road, and we were okay with that. We had full lives and ministries, were active with our church, and were all around really happy, content folks.

John and I became involved in the pro-life movement early in our marriage. And my interest in pro-life issues had begun to seriously grow ever since my second and third years of law school. Stemming from my pro-life passion was an eagerness to advance the public-policy cause of adoption.

I learned about a Christian woman named DeeannaMarie Wallace. She had been involved in adoption for decades, both personally and as a calling to help other kids and families. She and her husband, Randy, had nine kids, seven of whom were adopted. She had mentored and supported countless Christian families throughout the adoption process, and her name kept coming up whenever I spoke with anyone about adoption.

Deeanna was developing a reputation as the Christian go-to lady on adoption. I needed to connect with her. Through a series of phone calls and various connections, Deeanna invited John and me to their home for dinner.

Unknown to us, that night would change our lives forever.

John and I held hands and said grace around the dinner table in Deeanna and Randy's modest home. Joining us were their five girls, who ranged in age from five to fifteen and represented every size, shape, color, ethnicity, and background. Several of the girls were already adopted; others were in the Wallace home through foster care.

"There are orphans right here in Hawaii who need adoptive families," Deeanna told us passionately. "They're trapped in foster care, and the church really needs to get involved."

We looked at their girls. Here they were, former legal orphans in our own state, our own community, our own neighborhood.

Throughout the course of the night, we learned that these girls had experienced abuse, neglect, and abandonment. Unspeakable, harrowing things were done to them by their birth parents, whose job it was to take care of and protect them. We also learned that if a child is in foster care long enough, eventually the birth-parents' rights will be terminated, and the child will become a "legal orphan." And then that child will sit and wait. And wait. And wait. And wait.

These kids wake up each day wondering if they'll have to pack up again and move to another foster home—for any or no reason. And there they'll sit, and if a loving adoptive family doesn't come into their lives, they'll turn eighteen and "age out" or exit the foster-care system. Those who do will likely become adults who belong nowhere and to no one.

Deeanna told us, "Every year in the United States, more than twenty thousand youth age out of the system. And not surprisingly, the statistics show that many of them end up in prison or at homeless shelters and receive government aid, and they sometimes have kids who also end up in foster care.

"In Hawaii," she continued, "there are twenty-five hundred kids in foster care. And hundreds are waiting to be adopted."

John and I were stunned. There were children needing families in our own backyard? Could this be true? We were two reasonably smart people who'd been completely ignorant about a really big problem. Near the end of the evening, Deeanna showed us a picture of some friends of hers—a military family who had six children, all through the blessing of adoption. Deeanna said we reminded her of them.

Honestly, I thought she must be nuts to think that.

My head was spinning. John and I were Christ followers. We knew that God's Word spoke frequently about God's heart for orphans and the Christian's duty to care for them. We had talked about adoption before, and we were always open to it, but we'd never pursued it seriously. We thought maybe it would happen after we had birth children. As pro-lifers, we'd always said we'd adopt any baby who would otherwise be aborted. That was a no-brainer.

Why would these kids in foster care be any different? How could we do nothing about what we'd heard? We'd been so blessed. We had room in our house. How could we turn our backs on kids in need?

We weren't sure what we were going to do, but we knew we had to do something. Hearing about the needs of these kids awakened John's sense of protection. He's a military man, after all, and he couldn't just sit back and not take action. He had to do something!

I kept thinking about the Good Samaritan in Luke 10:25–37. Remember the story? Jesus told a parable about a Jewish man traveling from Jerusalem to Jericho who gets attacked. He's beaten, robbed, and left for dead.

A priest happens to be walking down the same road, but when he sees the man, he passes by on the other side. Another man comes along, but again, he passes by on the other side. Then a Samaritan comes down the road, and when he sees the injured man, he takes pity on him. He bandages the man's wounds. Then he puts the man on his own donkey and takes him to an inn. The next day he pays the innkeeper and says, "Look after him . . . and when I return, I will reimburse you for any extra expense you may have" (verse 35).

I sensed that God was challenging us, asking us if, like the religious men in the parable, we'd just pass by and do nothing. Or would we be like the Samaritan, who did something about the person in need right in front of him?

John and I talked and prayed about it *a lot*.

It's hard to explain. Those of you who have been through this experience of responding to God's leading know what we mean. Those of you considering it are probably beginning to sense that compelling nudge. John and I have often said it feels as though God's hand is at your back, pushing you forward.

Talking and praying abstractly about the things that break God's heart is one thing. Seeing and hearing needs up close and personal—in your face, literally—is clarifying. There was no way we could see what we were seeing—precious faces, voices, and lives of real kids in desperate need—and go back to our comfortable life unchanged.

There was no noble decision making; it was just crystal clear to John and me that we were going to do something. We were completely on the same page, something we paid close attention to. It wasn't a hard decision; it was the obvious decision, set right before us. When we looked at the pros and cons, the obvious pros were that we were doing what Jesus commanded His followers to do and being who He commanded us to *be*. There weren't really any cons that could compete with that.

We were excited—thrilled, really. And scared. But we believed as we trusted the Lord with all our hearts, leaned not on our own understanding, and acknowledged Him in all our ways that He was directing our path (Proverbs 3:5-6).

As John and I processed what we had seen and heard at the Wallaces', we kept coming back to one of the girl's stories. Susie was a troubled teenage girl. All of her other siblings were in separate foster homes, and she didn't get to see them very often.

This is common in foster care and struck us as horribly sad. Imagine being removed from the only life you've known, even with its abuse and neglect, and not being able to communicate with your siblings, who might very well have been your only support because of your parents' deficiencies.

A judge colleague of mine often told the story of a little boy in foster care who told the judge he didn't believe in God. When the judge asked him why, the little boy said, "Because I pray every night to God to let me see my brother who is in another foster home. But I never get to, and my social worker says it's because there aren't enough people to drive me. If there was a God, He could get enough drivers."

Susie had one sister she wanted to see on a regular basis but wasn't able to. The sister, Angie, was in a foster home across the island, and it just wasn't feasible to get the girls together very often.

"Can you even believe that?" John said to me. "That seems so sad; we should do something about it. We could drive them to their visits."

"Well, I don't see any reason she couldn't live with us," I said enthusiastically. "We could make sure she sees her sister most weekends."

It can't be that hard, I thought to myself.

So Deeanna and I agreed that I should start by at least meeting Angie.

———⚬∞⚬———

I met Angie with Deeanna at a Honolulu McDonald's. She was a beautiful eleven-year-old local girl with gorgeous brown skin, chocolate-brown eyes, and beautiful dark hair. She was medium height, with a slight frame, and was completely adorable. I was crazy for her from the start. She seemed sweet and fidgety as Deeanna interacted with her playfully and skillfully. Unknown to Angie, our plans for her to live with us were already in the works. Deeanna had talked to her social worker and gotten permission for Angie to be placed in our home.

I asked her questions, and she smiled sweetly, looking me directly in the eyes. Later, I told John, "I think she likes me. We really hit it off!"

We were going to be foster parents! What an adventure. We were so excited.

We had just moved from a rental place on the east side of Oahu into our very own home on the far west side. The house had four bedrooms, and as we had moved in, John and I told the Lord He could fill it up as He saw fit. Having Angie in our home seemed like the beginning of that answer to our prayers. Even though we hadn't been to foster-care training yet, we could get a criminal background check done and secure a "specific child license" to care for Angie.

After that first near-perfect meeting with Angie concluded, Deeanna and I stayed at McDonald's to talk further.

I was so jazzed, I could hardly stay in my seat. My mind was whirling. We could do this. We could really help this precious girl have a great life. *She'll get to see her sister regularly. We'll take her to church. We'll show her what good parents can be like. We'll love her. It'll be fun. We'll adopt her if she needs a permanent family. She can go to college, meet a great Christian man, our grandkids will be gorgeous . . .* Deeanna's voice interrupted my mental ramblings.

"You know, Kelly," she said very slowly in her sweet, wonderful way, "this could be really hard. Because of the trauma Angie has faced, she won't be easy to parent. I really want to make sure you know what you're getting into." She was so serious as she sat there staring at me. Deeanna is a teensy thing, about one hundred pounds soaking wet, but with the quiet determination and strength of a herd of bulls.

You know the muffled sound adults make in those Charlie Brown shows? *Wha wha wha wha wha* . . . That's all I heard as Deeanna talked.

I smiled back at her and wondered why she was droning on about how hard this could be. John and I had listened to plenty of *Focus on the Family* broadcasts and other shows about how important it was to be in charge, set limits, dare to discipline, and so on. I was sure we'd be good parents.

John and I are rather competent people, I thought. *I mean, come on, I'm a lawyer. I've done hard things. Law school. The bar exam. John's in the air force. He's a military man, guarding our country. He has a degree in business. He's been working on the business-services side of the air force his entire career. Why is Deeanna being so skeptical?* I wondered and just kept smiling.

When the questions and lecture finally ended, I asked, "When can I pick her up?"

"Today at three thirty. You can pick her up after school," Deeanna replied, a huge smile breaking across her face as she sat back in her seat, keenly aware that nothing she said would matter at this point.

"I'm picking her up after school!" I told John on the phone, half squealing from delight and anticipation. He was thrilled and got permission to leave work early so we could go together to pick up our new foster daughter.

It was really happening.

We drove to the very far west side of the island, following directions back toward the mountain to her school. I had the paperwork from the social worker, and when the class let out, there we were waiting for Angie.

She looked at me with complete surprise and said, "It's you. It's really you." She smiled and gave me a hug. I introduced her to John, who opened the door for her and ushered us all into the car.

When I asked Angie what she'd love to do more than anything, she said she wanted to go to an arcade. We were happy to comply. We drove to the local arcade and soon Angie was surrounded by lots of noise and flashing lights, having a blast.

She asked if she could call me Mom. I swooned. "Of course you can call me Mom," I said as I hugged her.

And John was now Dad. He glowed. We had a real dinner together as a family. We thanked God.

"She can finally see an example of a godly dad," I told John later. Her birth father was in prison at the time.

"This is amazing," we told each other. "What an honor to be used by God to help an abused girl in foster care. Kingdom adventures are fabulous. Why didn't we do this earlier? Why don't more people do this?"

And so we were off on our grand adventure. It seemed like a beautiful dream.

2

Tempted to Give Up

The dream lasted about three days, and then it began to unravel into one of the darkest nightmares of our lives. Sounds crazy and melodramatic, I know. How bad could it have been, right? She was only eleven and about sixty pounds.

But that's what happened. And all in a very short amount of time.

The details are a bit fuzzy in my mind, but the trauma lingers just a tad even at this writing, ten years later. It went something like this.

The public school in our district was considered quite subpar, so we enrolled Angie in a private school nearby. Her social worker and guardian ad litem (the special lawyer appointed by the court to represent her) seemed to think we hung the moon for enrolling her in a private school. It just seemed like an obvious choice for us. We wanted the best for her.

I worked closely with the school, doing all kinds of mom stuff for the first time. It felt really good being responsible for Angie and taking care of her. I liked this mom thing. So far so good.

It didn't take long before we found out that Angie was dramatically behind in school. She was in fourth grade but could barely do first-grade work in many areas. And this was despite the fact that she was clearly a bright girl. All the abuse and neglect had taken a toll on her ability to learn or to even attend school regularly.

The administrators and teaching staff at the private school were amazing in how they worked with us. The teacher's daughter even became friends with Angie. *What a blessing!* I thought. But after about one week, Angie began to be completely disrespectful and defiant at home. At first it started leaking out a little at a time, but very quickly it escalated, affecting every single interaction. It didn't matter how we responded or how much discipline we imposed. Nothing helped.

Angie began to steal regularly and curse often. She constantly lied to us. And I don't mean little white lies; this was some serious crazy lying. Let me give you an example. One time Angie was standing in front of me, and she turned off the light. I said, "Honey, please turn the light back on." She started freaking out and said, "I didn't turn off the light."

Remember, I was standing there watching her turn off the light. "Honey, I don't mind that you turned the light off, and you're not in trouble. Please just turn it back on," I said calmly.

Twenty minutes of her screaming ensued, with her insisting, "I never turned off the light! Why are you such a liar, accusing me of that? I never touched the *#&* light."

I watched her turn off the light. I didn't care that she turned it off, and she wasn't in trouble for turning it off. What in the world was going on?

It soon became apparent that she detested me. She was rude and defiant at every turn, constantly screaming at me. She was spiteful and called me names, yelling that she hated me. I would stay calm as long as I was able, but then I would blow and yell right back at her. Very mature on my part, I know.

At other times I would ask her to do something simple, such as clearing her plate.

"Why do you hate me? You're such a *@#! I won't do it!" She'd throw her plate and then shut herself in her closet, refusing to come out.

I would pick her up at school, and she would ignore me. She would tell me not to show up publicly with her because she was embarrassed of me. She was playing volleyball after school. I had played volleyball in college. I thought that common interest might help us bond. But in all public settings, she either ignored me or was cruel. She would be polite to all other adults but could barely bring herself to interact with me except with rudeness.

I'd never had anything close to a temper in my life, but now there were moments I hated this girl. What in the world was the matter with me? Why wasn't this working?

While Angie was as mean as a rattlesnake to John and me—although not at the same time (I'll come back to that)—she would meet some stranger and be the most charming and delightful girl you'd ever seen.

Just like the girl I'd met in McDonald's the first time.

Trying to explain what was happening at home to someone with only a casual connection to her would have made us seem like flat-out liars. "She's so cute and polite and bright," everyone would say. Just like we did— before we lived with her.

Angie also tried to create a wedge between John and me by constantly telling one of us that the other was mean to her. One weekend John took her to the local Hawaiian palace. She was Hawaiian, and the palace was a great source of pride. He was trying to forge a connection through her interests and background. I could tell John was frazzled when he got home. He went upstairs, and Angie plunked down near me, sulking.

"How was it?" I asked.

"Horrible. Dad was so mean to me. He grabbed my arm for no reason, and it really hurt." She pouted. If I hadn't lived with her and had a clear understanding of what she was like, I might have believed her. She could be extremely convincing. I told her I was sorry she didn't have a good time, but I made it clear I didn't believe for one minute that John did anything like what she had described.

I looked her in the eye and told her not to bother going there with me. Thankfully, her turn-one-against-the-other strategy never got her anywhere with either of us, but she tried hard.

As I was lying in John's arms later that evening, he told me the true story of how she'd acted that day—more of the same rudeness, defiance, lying, and scheming. We were both worn out and nearing our breaking point. We began to think seriously about the repercussions if she lied to the social worker about us. She lied about everything. Would they believe us?

Angie's horrific behavior and our constantly negative interactions with her were consuming our lives. We knew in our heads about her horrible past. We knew this way of life was all she'd ever known, but we were numb by this point.

Our interactions with her were so maddening that both of us began to turn into versions of ourselves we barely recognized. We loved our life before, and we hated our life now. We had ruined it. No, she had ruined it.

I also called Deeanna constantly. Poor Deeanna. She had tried to warn me, but I hadn't listened. Now I was constantly crying to her and asking her what in the world to do. She was such a faithful friend and counselor, but the hard truth was that Angie was a very disturbed girl, and we were quickly reaching the end of our rope.

But something else was happening with both John and me that ran counter to our other strong feelings. The Lord was giving us a fierce determination not to give up. We were reminded about all the adults in Angie's life who had given up on her and failed her and gotten her to this point. We were truly miserable, yes, but we were determined not to quit.

During this time I was researching everything I could get my hands on and came across one psychological book on kids who have been through trauma. The book included a checklist for something called reactive attachment disorder.

Randy and Deeanna had tried to talk to us about this on that night we had dinner with them. And what had we called it in our minds? Oh yeah, *psychobabble*. But now as I read the checklist of symptoms, I could see that it fit Angie to a tee. We weren't going crazy! John and I rejoiced. Angie had a real problem. Now all we needed was a real solution.

But that didn't come so easily. All the books I read were long on symptoms but short on practical advice for how we could live day to day in a way that would make any of this better for her and for us.

About that time I found out from the social worker that Angie had a history of violence, including pulling out knives and hurting animals. We realized just how serious the situation was and how ill-equipped we were to help her.

One day she did something even worse than her usual defiance, lying, yelling, stealing, or cursing. I truly can't even remember what it was. But I remember it was a breaking point, and John and I just needed some space from her. That's when Deeanna showed up to take Angie for the weekend so we could have some time to think. We needed to reflect. To go back to the beginning. Back to when God brought John and me together. Back to the parts of our lives we could be sure about.

3

Looking Back

Looking back, John and I can see how our journey toward foster care and adoption started way before we ever realized it. We first met at a weekend volleyball tournament in Omaha, Nebraska. I'd just moved to Omaha to attend law school at Creighton University after graduating from Marquette University in Milwaukee, Wisconsin. John was in the air force and was heading up the volleyball team that I would be a part of.

I don't remember whether our team won or lost most of the matches, but somehow through the course of conversation that day, John and I figured out that we were both Christians. By day's end, we had a date to go to church together the next morning.

That was September 29, 1990. We were married August 24, 1991.

During that year of dating, I learned that John was from North Providence, Rhode Island. He joined the air force when he was twenty-one years old, and Omaha was his second official assignment. His father and mother both lived in Rhode Island, although they had divorced when John was a teenager. He also had two brothers.

While we were dating, John and I realized how compatible we were. He's intensely introverted but so socially skilled, you'd never know it. I'm the extrovert. Our personalities seemed to balance each other very well. We found that we had similar interests and spent our time together going to movies, hiking, eating out, attending church activities, playing or watching sports, and discussing politics. We both had an appreciation for beautiful outdoor scenery and enjoyed taking long car rides together. I learned that John could be both funny and melancholy, and that he was a faithful and kind man.

The first Thanksgiving after we got acquainted, John and I met each other's families. My parents had divorced when I was in high school and were both remarried by this time. After visiting John's brother and sister-in-law in Chicago that day, John and I decided to make the three-hour drive to my hometown of Wisconsin Dells, Wisconsin, to surprise my dad and his wife. Soon after, John met my mother and her husband. There was a clear consensus among my relatives: John was a great guy.

Shortly before John and I met, I recommitted my life to God, after not having given Him the time of day since grade school. John and I had made a decision a few months into our dating relationship that we wanted our faith in Christ to be the foundation of our relationship, and we were excited about growing together in this area of our lives.

A respect and passion for the sanctity of human life had always been part of my life, even when God wasn't in my conscious thought. I was thrilled that John shared this passion. For him, it was just intuitive.

For me, the reality of the gift of life was ingrained in my experience. My mom was only sixteen years old when she became pregnant with me. She'd always planned on going to college. She'd been reading news and business magazines since junior high, and a bright future in business awaited her. But that vision for her future was set aside when she dropped out of high school, got her GED, married my dad, and became my teenage mother. My brother came along less than two years later, and to this day, I marvel at the amazing job she did as such a young mother.

Abortion hadn't been legalized at the time she became pregnant with me, but there were still ways for it to happen. I asked her once if she ever considered it, and she said, "Absolutely not."

I think of what the prevailing wisdom of the world would be today for a teenage girl pregnant out of wedlock with a bright future ahead of her. The answer seems so simple: Get rid of the problem and return to life as planned.

But thankfully, my mom chose to have me, and to this day I'm reminded of the magnificent gift of life.

The day after John and I were married, we drove eight hours from Wisconsin back to Nebraska. Instead of going on a honeymoon, I started my second year of law school at a brand-new university two days after our wedding. I had just turned twenty-three years old, and John was twenty-nine.

It was a crazy time of change—new marriage, new law school, new daily two-hour round-trip commute. But it was a great time, too. We made time for road trips, eating out, and watching movies together. We also plugged in to a wonderful church in Omaha. We taught Sunday school to preschoolers and began to get more involved in the pro-life movement.

The pro-life movement we became part of also emphasized the importance of valuing the lives of the elderly. It saddened us to learn that elderly folks are often neglected and alone. We regularly visited nursing homes and became the only companions for a lonely eighty-two-year-old man named Ed. Ed had no family other than his eighty-five-year-old sister, Ruth. So we became his family, visiting as often as we could to talk, laugh, play games, and just be present in his life.

During my second and third years of law school, I became involved with Christian legal groups and grew even more interested in the issues of life, religious liberty, and public policy. I'll never forget the first time our group of Christian law students decided to speak up in defense of religious freedom before the Nebraska legislature. I planned to testify at a committee hearing and make the case for religious freedom in the workplace. Even though the hearing was weeks away, once I knew I was going to do it, I was so nervous I couldn't sleep.

But when the day of the hearing finally arrived, I was ready. I had prepared and then prepared some more by researching, writing, and memorizing my points. So instead of being nervous, I was excited to make my case to lawmakers. That was when it happened. I was bit by the public-policy bug. Most people either love or hate being involved in public policy. I loved it and knew it would become a big part of my future.

Speaking up for the poor and needy became both my passion and vocation. By God's grace, I graduated from law school with distinction and immediately began the dreadful task of studying for the bar exam. After passing the bar, I went to work for a Nebraska state senator who championed the issues John and I cared so much about. I learned the inner workings of the legislative process—how our laws are made. I was part of it from the inside, and I loved it.

During this time John was faithfully laboring away in the air force. After I'd worked in the state capitol for almost a year, John had the opportunity to transfer to an air force recruiting squadron in Milwaukee, Wisconsin, just two hours from where most of my family lived. We prayed about it and decided to take the assignment. My father and his wife had two small children, my sister and brother, so we were looking forward to living closer to them. John's brother and his wife were also only a few hours away in Chicago. We couldn't pass up the chance to be nearer to our family.

I got a job with a state representative at the capitol in Madison, eighty miles from where John worked. So we bought a little house in the middle—well, actually, much closer for me. John bore the brunt of a long commute in an old car that barely kept him heated during the viciously cold Wisconsin winters.

A year after working in the Wisconsin legislature, I was offered a job as Director of Government Affairs at a trade association representing twenty or so health-insurance companies. For those of you who didn't catch it, "Director of Government Affairs" is a euphemism for the dreaded "L" word: lobbyist. Accepting this position would make me both a lawyer and a lobbyist—not the most popular of folks.

But John and I prayed and felt a peace about my taking the job. So I worked as a lobbyist in Madison while John worked with his recruiting squadron in Milwaukee. After a couple of years, though, we faced a dilemma. John was at the point in his air force career where he would be sent involuntarily on a one-year tour of duty overseas without me if he didn't volunteer for an overseas tour of duty for three years (which would enable me to go with him).

A year without each other was unthinkable to us, and so John began to research where we could be transferred for three years. Interestingly, both Hawaii and Alaska were possibilities, which was great because I could still practice law if I wanted to.

Even though we figured everyone in the air force would be applying for the Hawaii position, we threw our hat in the ring anyway. For months we would pop popcorn and watch *Hawaii Five-0* in our little Lake Mills home, dreaming about the crazy fantasy of being transferred to Hawaii. To be honest, I had never been out of the continental United States. I didn't even know Hawaii was more than one island, a very embarrassing thing to admit.

I'll never forget the moment John called me at my office in Madison to tell me we were moving to Hawaii. It was November of 1997. I screamed at my desk, and my colleagues came running in to see what was wrong. We were Hawaii bound. Land of aloha, here we come!

4

Assignment: Paradise

That first Thanksgiving in Hawaii, we had pineapple stuffing with our turkey dinner in the restaurant of our gorgeous military hotel on Waikiki Beach. We thought we'd died and gone to heaven. The sand, the ocean, the views—it was almost more than we could take in. Our hotel room, which doubled as our new residence for the next couple of weeks, overlooked the ocean and the world-renowned Diamond Head crater. Every day we were looking at a sky-blue ocean and velvety-green mountains.

The air was moist but not hot. Slightly balmy but with a cool breeze. And when the sun set, the city lights were resplendent and thrilling. We would walk on the beach and watch the sunset. It was surreal. The beauty of it was intoxicating, and we wondered why in the world anyone would ever leave this place. We could see the airplanes leaving Honolulu International Airport, and we joked about those poor folks who had to leave our newfound paradise. We didn't want to leave anytime soon, if ever. We were just so happy.

It didn't take long, however, to realize that no place is perfect, and Honolulu was no exception.

John started his new job the Monday after Thanksgiving, which left me to find a place for us to live—and eventually, a job. Reality set in.

Unlike apartment buildings on the U.S. mainland, the ones in Hawaii were independently owned. I couldn't just stop by a building to check on vacancies. The process was overwhelming and reduced me to tears on multiple occasions. I didn't know and couldn't pronounce any of the street names or areas of Honolulu. Kalanianaole Highway, Makiki, Kaimuki, Kahala, Kapahulu, Kamehameha Avenue—you get the picture. Where in the world would we live? The places I visited that we could afford seemed old, run-down, and gross. I was not a happy camper.

Finally, after several weeks we found a teensy little apartment on the thirty-fourth floor of a Waikiki high-rise. By the time our household goods arrived from Wisconsin, there was almost no room to move around in our six-hundred-square-foot, one-bedroom apartment that cost more than most houses on the mainland. My tears were flowing regularly at this point.

What were we doing all alone on this dot in the middle of the Pacific Ocean, five thousand miles from our families?

Once we were finally settled into our postage-stamp-sized apartment, I was ready to find a job. I really wanted to become involved in pro-life and pro-family issues again. Before we'd left Wisconsin, I found out that a new nonprofit organization called the Hawaii Family Forum had been established and was searching for an executive director. I'd tracked down the contact information for the chairman, Mr. Lee.

I called Mr. Lee and told him who I was and asked for a meeting. He obliged, and before long I was stumbling through downtown Honolulu to meet with this prominent Japanese Christian businessman who headed an international architectural firm.

I was so nervous I thought I might be ill. Hawaii seemed more like another country than the fiftieth state in the U.S. Everything was different—the people, the architecture, the food, the smells. It was dizzying.

As I waited in the lobby of the architectural firm, Mr. Lee's assistant was so kind and chatted with me until he arrived. Mr. Lee was proper and serious, and I felt like a giant at five foot ten looking down at him. But he was kind, and we had an engaging conversation about the vision and plans for the Hawaii Family Forum (HFF). Everything sounded just right to me, but Mr. Lee felt I would be the wrong person to head up the organization because I was a newcomer and didn't know the community. At this point, I couldn't even pronounce the names of streets!

Mr. Lee pointed out that Hawaii was a very close-knit and unique community and that the board of directors was looking for a retired Kamaaina (local) man with lots of community connections to run the organization. I understood his reasoning but was quite disappointed. I felt that God was leading me back into the world of family advocacy and that HFF was where He wanted me. But it was clear that Mr. Lee had reached a different conclusion.

During this time, John and I found a wonderful church, Kaimuki Christian Church, whose pastor was from Nebraska and loved football. Those connections with home were extremely comforting to us. The first day we visited the church, we sat down, opened the bulletin, and saw an insert for what else? Hawaii Family Forum's search for an executive director. We truly believed the Lord was confirming this as my future role, but it seemed the organization's board members hadn't received the same message.

So John and I decided to wait.

Much to my relief, one of the health-care companies I represented in Wisconsin put in a good word for me with a counterpart in Hawaii, and I was hired to write position papers and conduct research for the company's lobbyists. On my second day at work, one of the lobbyists quit, and I was thrown into a whole new world—the Hawaii legislature.

In addition to lobbying for the health-care company, I kept track of legislative bills I thought would be of interest to the Hawaii Family Forum. I would call Mr. Lee in the evenings and give him all the information. After several weeks, I also met several other members of the HFF board of directors through a series of coincidences. I introduced myself and told each of them about my moonlighting efforts on their behalf. I also learned that after nearly nine months of searching, they still hadn't hired an executive director.

A short time later I received a call from Mr. Lee asking me to come in for an interview with the entire board. I was psyched. This was my dream job, and the Lord was finally answering my prayers. The board offered me the position shortly after my interview, and I gladly accepted.

Hawaii was the first state to become embroiled in the same-sex marriage controversy, and my tenure began with this high-profile issue. I appeared in the media and was involved in public-education efforts to maintain the legal definition of marriage as being between one man and one woman. After a seemingly endless campaign to defend marriage, we awaited the results of a critical vote in the fall of 1998. Almost 70 percent of the people of Hawaii voted for traditional marriage. It wasn't even close.

Our staff at the Hawaii Family Forum worked on many other issues in the legislature and in the media, some of them controversial, some of them not. We were passionate about upholding the sanctity of human life and human dignity. We also worked with the medical-and-disability-rights communities to stop the legalization of physician-assisted suicide and with the feminist community to pass better protections for children victimized by commercial sexual exploitation.

But another passion was stirring within me. I really wanted to work on the issue of adoption—professionally, that is. As a strong pro-life advocate, I wanted to know what barriers could be removed to better advance the cause of adoption. That was when I met Dee-anna Wallace, and our lives got a little crazy.

Let me tell you, John and I had no idea what we were getting into—or that in just a few short weeks, Angie would turn our lives upside down.

5

Saying Yes to God

While Angie was with Deeanna that weekend, John and I went around and around about what to do.

"We are not kicking her out. We won't abandon her or give up on her," John insisted. I had to agree, despite my feelings.

"I know," I replied. "She's had a horrible life, and right now we're her only chance."

"If we as Christians don't help her, who will?" John pointed out. "How will she have a chance at success in life?"

The biggest blessing during this time was the gift of unity God gave to John and me. We could and did talk for hours about His assignment to care for Angie, and we came to the same conclusions every time.

One of the books we'd been reading advised parents to teach their kids to say "I don't want to, but I will" when they're asked to do something they'd rather not do, such as picking up their toys. This approach allows children to be honest and express their feelings (I don't want to) while teaching them to comply with the directives of parents or other authority figures (but I will).

That's where John and I landed that weekend.

We told the Lord "We don't want to, but we will" when it came to taking Angie back and sticking it out with her. We said yes to God even though we were still experiencing emotional anguish over the situation. The rest of the weekend, we prepared the house for her return. We absorbed all the advice we could find in books and resources, made a plan, and braced for the next round with Angie.

By this time, the social worker already knew what had been happening. Angie had demanded that we let her call the social worker regularly so she could tell her how horrible we were. We had happily given Angie the phone each time, and when she was done talking, we let the social worker know how tenuous this placement was.

Angie had also continued threatening that she would demand to be moved, and we had secretly rejoiced at the prospect.

At the end of the weekend that Angie spent with Deeanna, we said we would take Angie back, but first she had a simple choice to make: Did she want to apologize and come home or not? We had forgiven her and would welcome her home. All she needed to do was say she was sorry.

John and I held our collective breath as we waited for Angie's response. She demanded to be moved to a different foster home.

It was over.

To be honest, we were so thankful. We could get our lives back! The relief was immediate. But we were also completely and utterly spent. We were emotionally wiped out. As I write this, it seems silly that just one month with an eleven-year-old was so devastating, but I truly believe we were experiencing some form of post-traumatic stress.

Angie lived with us the month of May 2000. After she moved out, John and I barely left the house for the next few months, except for work. We spent a lot of time together in our backyard, figuratively licking our wounds. We prayed, read the Bible, and talked a lot about what in the world happened to us. We had lots of questions for God, and for a while, we were rather adamant that we'd never—I mean never *ever*—be foster parents again.

What a disaster.

But by the end of the summer, the Lord had once again been working in both of our hearts. No matter how traumatized we felt, how could we just turn our backs on the needs of kids because it was hard and painful? If we as Christians couldn't handle the difficulties of helping these kids, what would happen to them? Who else would help them? Now that we knew more about attachment problems and other challenges common to kids in foster care, couldn't we do better?

John and I settled on a plan: We would take the route of prospective missionaries. We would make ourselves available to the Lord and just see what happened.

6

The Journey Home

After much discussion and prayer, we decided that rather than providing temporary foster care, we would pursue adoption through foster care. We'd concentrate on helping the kids who were almost certainly going to need an adoptive family. And we thought we'd care for a younger child this time, maybe a toddler.

However difficult our experience had been with Angie, it didn't negate the fact that there were kids who needed families, and we felt God calling us to fill this role. Of course, we were rather terrified from our Angie experience, but God had made it clear to us that this was the path He was leading us on. So we read more and tried to get better prepared for future difficulty.

To qualify as adoptive parents through foster care, we had to take an eight-week foster-care training class, complete a home study, and make sure our criminal clearance and medical records were current.

We felt as if we were just plodding along, no longer bubbling with excitement, but we truly believed we were where God wanted us and were being obedient to Him. Each Thursday I dreaded the training class. It seemed unhelpful, and the things that were described sure didn't match the experience we'd just had. We really didn't think we'd be foster parents again anytime soon, but we both felt that God wanted us to be there.

Then came the home study or, as John calls it, the full-cavity search. This sweet, young woman came to our home and asked us all kinds of intrusive questions.

"Tell me about your childhood," she'd begin. "How often do you talk to your parents? Did you ever experience abuse as a child? How will you discipline? How's your marriage? How often do you floss?" Okay, that last question wasn't part of the interview, but it felt as if she wanted to know absolutely everything about us. Though I understood why she needed to ask so many questions, it just felt wrong for her to be so nosy.

Going through this kind of interrogation was stressful. There was so much on the line. We kept worrying, *What if we answer something wrong?*

But at the end of the day, this pain-in-the-neck part of the process was doable. We didn't enjoy it, but we got through it. And I believe God used it to change and grow John and me and prepare us for what was ahead. Put another way: If you can't handle the process, the kids are gonna eat your lunch.

If you're a type-A control freak, like I was, adoption through foster care (or adoption of any type) is going to be very, very difficult. You have no control. This was hard for me. But through it all, God taught me much more deeply that He is in control, and I need to learn to trust Him with my life.

The truth is, I learned many of those lessons through flat-out failure as I floundered and fretted the entire time. Instead of praying, I worried. Instead of trusting, I called Deeanna constantly with a steady stream of complaints about the process. Instead of waiting on God, I called social workers and guardians ad litem far more often than I should have, which probably wasn't productive. Too often I lived in the stress of it all instead of living in the peace God provides for such situations in life.

Thankfully, God is patient and kind, even if we have to learn the hard way sometimes.

———∞———

During our time of preparation, Deeanna made a very good suggestion. "Well, Kelly, if you're going to be parents, you might want to get some practice. I know a baby boy in foster care who needs respite care," she said. She went on to explain that the boy's foster mom was leaving the island on vacation and couldn't take him along. The foster mom needed someone to take care of him for a few days.

Hmm, practice, I thought, *not a bad idea.*

To be honest, I didn't really think we'd need practice. This was a baby, right? How hard could it be to take care of a baby? Amazingly, I think John and I still had very unrealistic ideas about what it takes to be good parents—something I've noticed is quite common for couples without kids. After listening to *Focus on the Family* for years and hearing countless sermons on parenting, we were quite confident, thank you very much, that we would do quite well.

No, we would never be lax on discipline; we'd never issue countless empty threats without consequences; we'd never let our lives revolve unhealthily around our children's wants and desires. And if we learned anything from our first foster experience, it was that we would do things right from the start so our children wouldn't end up like Angie.

As I think of those early days, I just shake my head at our arrogance and thank God for His patience.

It was August, and we wouldn't be bringing a child home until the following spring according to our timetable, so we weren't in any hurry. But thankfully, even with our unfounded parenting confidence, we realized that we could, in fact, use the practice. Practice sounded sensible and logical. I called the foster mom, Debbie, mentioned that my friend Deeanna told me about her need, and offered to help.

She suggested I come to her home in Kaneohe on the other side of the island to meet her and the little guy, Daniel. She told me that he wasn't quite six months old and had been born with symptoms of crystal methamphetamine addiction. His birth mother was a teenager who had used drugs and alcohol during her pregnancy. This little guy, Debbie told me, screamed for hours on end, especially every time he was in a car.

She said he was receiving occupational and physical therapy because he was developmentally delayed in many areas. She also said that his doctor and state child-welfare officials were concerned about possible brain damage resulting from his birth mother's drug and alcohol use during pregnancy, so they had scheduled a brain scan to better understand the extent of the damage.

With Debbie's trip coming up soon, we made arrangements for my visit. It was August 22, 2000—my thirty-second birthday. I drove through the gorgeous Ko'olau Mountains on my way to Kaneohe, praising God for the beauty of the islands and for the chance to help this lady I didn't know.

I also had absolutely no idea what the Lord was about to do in our lives. In a word, I was oblivious.

The house was tucked away in the mountains and was built

on stilts along a steep incline. It was an old house, as is common in Hawaii, and seemed quite run down. There were old cars, bikes, washing machines, and dryers lining the driveway. Not my cup of tea, as I prefer clean, tidy, and new.

I was apprehensive and felt an icky, unidentifiable feeling. Making my way through the clutter to the front door, I knocked nervously. Debbie appeared at the door and greeted me. She was pleasant enough, but very no-nonsense. There was nothing warm and fuzzy about her. I sensed no joy but rather a sad heaviness. She seemed overwhelmed. She barked orders at one of the older kids and sent a five-year-old outside to ride her bike alone.

The whole scene felt depressing to me. The house was old and broken down and smelled odd. I was very uncomfortable in the unfamiliar surroundings. After some initial pleasantries, Debbie pointed to the middle of the living room and said rather flatly, "There he is."

He was unbelievably cute, with his brown eyes and brown skin. He was just lying there in a pale-blue onesie outfit looking up at me.

"What's his ethnicity?" I asked, curious about what ethnic combination would produce such a gorgeous baby.

"He's Korean, Hawaiian, Filipino, and Chinese," Debbie said.

"May I hold him?" I asked.

"Sure," she replied.

I was completely captivated and googly-eyed. As I picked him up and cuddled him against my chest, I was smitten with this little baby boy. I melted into baby talk and handled him as if he were porcelain. And as I held him close to my chest, he fell asleep on me, as if he were finally home where he belonged, with the mother he'd been waiting for.

His foster mom expressed great surprise that he fell asleep on me, and as he slept, I probed her to learn everything about him. It was as if the lawyer in me was cross-examining a witness. I needed to know every detail about the past, present, and future plans for this boy. I asked any question I could think of. She probably really wanted me to be quiet, but I couldn't. I had to know everything.

At the end of our visit, I learned that this boy sleeping on my chest needed a forever family. His foster mom seemed very conflicted about not being able to adopt him, which felt awkward for me because now I found myself desperately wanting this little guy whom she seemed to want too. Debbie had several birth children, including two teenage girls and another baby boy from foster care whom she was planning to adopt.

She felt that Daniel needed to be with a family that had more time to devote to his special needs. She also felt she wouldn't be able to give him the attention he deserved, even though she cared about him. So even though she wasn't a warm and fuzzy foster mom, she was still deeply concerned for his well-being.

While Debbie was talking, something awakened in my heart in a dramatic and inexplicable way. At that moment, I became a mother. This little baby boy was vulnerable and alone, and his future was uncertain. I wanted to fix all that. This sleeping, beautiful, brown boy whose heart was beating next to mine became my child in my heart and mind.

Of course, I was fully aware that these feelings meant absolutely nothing in legal terms. Even though Daniel's birth parents didn't seem to be in the picture, I knew they had legal rights until the courts officially terminated them. I also knew that child-welfare officials were in charge of Daniel's care and might have plans of their own for him.

None of my rational thoughts carried one bit of weight, though, when stacked against the feelings in my heart. All I really knew for sure was that I had just held my son, and he had slept for hours on his new and forever mother.

I didn't want to leave Daniel, and he whimpered a little when I did. I told Debbie I would call her that night about the respite. I also let her know that if Daniel needed a family, John and I wanted to be that family. I lobbied her to put in a good word for us with the social worker (I was an officially registered lobbyist, after all). I thought that would help since she had just witnessed how quickly Daniel and I bonded.

When I got to the car, I called Deeanna even before calling John. I told her I loved this baby and wanted to be his mother. We discovered through conversation that his social worker, who would make the decisions about his future, was someone Deeanna knew quite well. I begged her to put in a good word for us, and she agreed. She also gave me the social worker's name and number and told me to call her right away because we didn't know what plans might already be in the works for baby Daniel.

I was in overdrive mode now, ready to lobby and make my case to everyone who needed to be convinced that I was meant to be Daniel's mother.

Next I called John. (This was before there were laws against talking on cell phones while driving.) Bubbling over with excitement, I told him the whole story.

"Honey, I think I just met our son," I said, absolutely giddy.

"Tell me, tell me," John insisted.

"Daniel is so delicious, and he needs a family. He just slept in my arms. We really bonded. I can't wait for you to meet him."

"I'm in. When can I meet him? I can't believe this is happening! He might be the reason why we've been getting ready!" John's excitement only fueled my own enthusiasm. Our ninth wedding anniversary was coming up in two days—August 24, 2000—and we made plans to visit baby Daniel on that day.

As John describes it, he became a daddy the moment he met our son. His heart fell hard too. Father and son seemed to have an instant connection. We didn't know at the time that this doesn't always happen. He played a bouncy game with Daniel for hours and held, cuddled, and sang to him. From that first moment, John was the most hands-on, gentle, and loving father I had ever seen. It was so beautiful to watch, and seeing him in that role made me love him even more. He could never get enough time with Daniel. He was and is an attentive, involved, and wonderful dad.

Incredibly strong feelings of affection, longing, caring, and protection replaced the feelings we'd had of just plodding along while we attended the training classes and completed the home study. It was an emotional roller coaster. John and I had been at the bottom, and now we were on cloud nine.

Because we felt sure that we were meant to be Daniel's parents, we sensed a tremendous urgency to make that happen. Even though we knew intellectually and theologically that God was in control, it was a constant battle to walk that out in a practical way. Sometimes we did well; sometimes we didn't. It's hard to be patient when you're so ready to adopt a child you've fallen in love with. That night after our visit with Daniel, John and I agreed that we wanted to adopt him. I still needed to contact the social worker, and I was very, very nervous.

Since I was calling the social worker at night, I expected to get her voice mail and leave her a message. Instead, to my great surprise, I got a live person. My heart was beating fast, and I felt as though the entire future of our family depended on my lobbying abilities at that moment. I had to make the case and make it well.

When the social worker answered the phone, it hit me almost

immediately that she had a strong Southern accent—something pretty rare in the Aloha State. She came across very calm and unaffected to me. Her name was Veronica, and though John and I didn't know it at the time, she would play a huge role in our lives and future.

I apologized profusely for bothering her in the evening, letting her know I only meant to leave her a message. The way I rambled on probably made her roll her eyes. First, I explained that we had met this baby boy who needed an adoptive family, and that we were doing respite care for him. Then I told her that he had really bonded with us, and we wanted to be his parents.

"We already have a few families in mind for him, and he still needs a brain scan," she explained nonchalantly to me.

My heart sank. Other families? What other families? We already knew and loved Daniel. He knew us. We had bonded.

I started to panic.

"Have you been to your training classes?" she asked, giving me a glimmer of hope.

"Yes! Yes, we're almost done with training, and our home study is complete," I quickly responded.

That moment was a forceful reminder of the importance of timely obedience to the call of God. What would Veronica have said if I hadn't answered yes? But our preparations combined with Deeanna's and Debbie's support apparently convinced Veronica to consider our plan on the spot. Without ever saying she had changed her mind, she just started talking about the official next steps we needed to take.

The call ended well. Veronica exercised due diligence by reviewing all our home study and licensing documents and talking to Deeanna and Debbie. Just days after our conversation, she called to say she was approving the plan to spend the next few weeks transition-ing Daniel to our home, where we would proceed with what was called an *at-risk adoption*.

At risk meant that even though we could proceed with the adop-tion plan while caring for Daniel in our home, several legal steps were still pending that might jeopardize the adoption. The risk was that the adoption might not work out and that our hearts would break into a million little pieces.

Quite a risk! This at-risk adoption was an unbelievable experi-ence that led John and me into a deeper trust that God was firmly in control. I'm not saying it was easy. We had given our hearts to Daniel, but we still had to surrender to the sovereignty of God be-cause we had absolutely no control over the future. We knew about all the uncertainties of adopting Daniel, but it was impossible to guard our hearts from crushing disappointment if things didn't work out. Thankfully, God knew our naïveté and vulnerability, and He provided grace and mercy in abundance.

The next few weeks were a blur. The transition plan was to have Daniel gradually spend more time with John and me while he con-tinued living in the only environment he had ever known. Eventu-ally, he would be spending so much time with us that leaving Debbie's wouldn't be such a horrible shock to his little system.

I drove forty-five minutes each way nearly every day to hold my son, who almost always slept in my arms. I began to hate one of the most beautiful stretches of highway in America because I only wanted Daniel home with us and never wanted him to sleep any-where else ever again.

Debbie told me that she could tell Daniel knew in his little spirit that something was happening, because he cried for hours at night. He was probably very confused at this point. John and I prayed for and worried about him whenever he wasn't with us.

And then the day came when we would make that drive one last time. No more going back. No more sharing our son. He would finally be home forever. He, and we, would wait no more.

That day was Saturday, September 9, 2000. It was a surreal experience. We started the day as a childless couple having a meeting with our pastor and some friends about a new small group we were starting. We could barely concentrate, and at the end of the meeting, we told them we were going to pick up our son. In a few hours, our family of two would be a family of three—even if it wasn't legal yet.

John and I prayed and gave thanks to God for what was about to happen. As we drove to Debbie's, we drew closer to each other in our giddiness. When we finally arrived at the house, we quickly packed up Daniel's things. Debbie seemed conflicted about his leaving, perhaps knowing it was right but feeling sad nonetheless. We thanked her and her family for the role they had played in Daniel's life and ours.

When John and I got in the car with our new baby boy, just the three of us, we were elated and couldn't wait to put distance between the past without him and the here and now with him. We had a son! He screamed the whole way home, but that didn't faze us; we just wished we could make him feel better. We were so excited and a little scared, but mostly just thrilled to truly begin this next phase of life. We had no doubts whatsoever that God had made us a family. We already loved Daniel so much.

We took pictures of the first moment Daniel entered his new home. We were tired. We were happy. We were a family.

7

Full-Time, Frontline, Forever

As grateful as we were and are that Daniel's birth mother chose to give him life, her choice to use drugs and alcohol while pregnant frequently made us angry during those early days as we saw Daniel suffer the consequences. We went through a constant process of choosing to forgive her and being grateful for her choice for life.

Daniel has a small bump on his forehead from the trauma he suffered in the womb. Every night for years, while tucking Daniel into bed, John would kiss that mark two times, once for Daniel's birth father and once for his birth mother, whispering a silent prayer of forgiveness over their lives. Only by God's grace were we able to extend forgiveness to Daniel's birth parents. And God's grace and mercy continually remind us that we need forgiveness just like everyone else.

The drugs and alcohol Daniel had been exposed to in utero caused significant developmental delays. He wasn't hitting the typical developmental milestones for infants. And he had another serious physical challenge. Every muscle in his little body was tight and taut, and he had enormous sensory-stimulation issues. He would often scream at the slightest touch, as if the sensation was magnified far beyond what he could tolerate.

But it also seemed as if he knew he needed to be held. As long as I held him, he was happy, but if I put him down, he'd scream like nothing we'd ever heard before. We'd never heard Daniel scream because we'd always held him at Debbie's home, not only when we first met him, but through the entire transition period. When we took him home with us and real life set in, we had to set him down, have him nap, get him into a routine, and so on. But putting him down led to the high-pitched screams that shattered our nerves and seemed as if they could shatter glass.

Our nerves weren't the only things that shattered after we brought Daniel home. Once again, our cushy life crumbled before our eyes. We went from deciding which movie to watch or which coffee shop to visit to caring for a small, screaming, completely dependent baby. All new parents know the feeling. And those with colicky babies or babies exposed to drugs or alcohol know the amplified feeling.

As I mentioned, Daniel wanted me to hold him at all times. Suddenly I had no other use for my arms. Thanks to the flexibility of the Hawaii Family Forum board of directors, I was leading the organization from my home office now, wheeling and dealing with the legislature, talking to senators on the phone, and carrying Daniel. (Tragically, I didn't know about baby slings until later.)

Why couldn't I put him down and watch him coo like babies I'd seen on television? He would sleep soundly on me for hours at a time, but the second I'd try to put him down, he would immediately wake up and—you guessed it—begin screaming.

As you've probably gathered by now, I'm not a natural with

some of this parenting stuff. In fact, any supermom-types who are reading this may be completely baffled by what I'm about to confess: Daniel's constant screaming and his need to be held at all times were killing me.

I was home all day with our new baby boy while John was at work. He received countless calls from his frazzled wife telling him how hard everything was—the physical therapy, the occupational therapy, the appointments, but mostly the SCREAMING. I was a wreck. But John was consistently there for me during this time. He would encourage me over the phone, letting me vent and assuring me that things would be okay.

Shortly after we brought Daniel home, my mother flew to Hawaii and met her grandson for the first time. I had put Daniel down for a nap, and, of course, he was screaming. She assured me he would stop screaming and eventually fall asleep if I didn't give in but let him cry it out instead.

The screaming went on for hours, and Daniel never stopped. He never fell asleep. When we needed to leave the house, I finally had to pick him up. The minute I did, he stopped crying.

I remember calling John one day in tears and asking him, "What if this never changes?" He tried to reassure me and calm me down. Don't get me wrong. We were madly in love with Daniel. I remember how, despite everything, we'd wake up every morning wanting to see him first thing because we'd missed him during the night. Just writing this makes me chuckle.

And John . . . well, you just never saw such a great daddy. He rushed home from work every day and couldn't get enough playtime with Daniel. It was a beautiful thing to behold.

After a couple of months, Daniel started to become more independent and scream less. I was so thrilled. Finally, he could entertain himself, and I got my arms back. I was beginning to feel normal again.

Occupational therapy helped tremendously with Daniel's developmental progress, and after several months, he was on track. A therapist would come to the house to work with him, and I did baby massage and other exercises with him regularly during the day. Daniel began to catch up developmentally, hitting age-appropriate milestones like sitting, crawling, and grasping at objects.

Soon we were developing what seemed like a more normal schedule. In fact, when I read about baby development, Daniel seemed to be ahead of schedule in reaching certain milestones related to independence.

John and I were cruising along in life, feeling pretty happy once again. We took lots of walks, pushing Daniel in the stroller and thanking God for our happy little family.

8

A Divine
Appointment

O nce you enter the adoption world, it's common to stay
connected with those who have journeyed with you or
have journeyed through it themselves. Deeanna became
one of my best friends, and we were in touch with her regularly. We
tried to help with her desire to educate other prospective adoptive
parents and support those who'd already adopted. This was Deeanna's passion and calling in life.

A key part of that calling was to help provide the very special-
ized training and support these adoptive families would need to effectively parent their hurting and challenging children. To accomplish this, Deeanna would occasionally invite experts from the U.S.
mainland to come to Hawaii to provide training for families. When
this happened, those of us in the group shared the responsibility of
hosting the expert for lunch or dinner.

On one such occasion, a woman who had successfully parented
many incredibly challenging, even violent, children came to the island to encourage and train adoptive families. She wasn't a medical

doctor, psychologist, or psychiatrist, but as an adoptive parent, she'd lived through the joys and traumas, rather than just watching others do it. In the process, she had learned some incredibly important lessons the hard way.

Our informal network of adoptive families took turns hosting her for meals, and John and I were scheduled to take her to lunch one Sunday afternoon. We were tired and really, really, really didn't want to do it. But it was one of those times when we needed to keep our commitment no matter how we felt.

We met the woman and her adult daughter at one of the most beautiful restaurants on the beach, just outside Waikiki in the spectacular area of Kahala. Of course, our precious Daniel was with us, and he sat on my lap holding his bottle while John and I chatted with the woman about our experiences to date.

She asked me how long Daniel had been holding his own bottle.

"Awhile, I guess," I said proudly. I went on to say how great this was, especially since he'd had some developmental delays.

Then I explained that Daniel had finally become more independent and would do things on his own, which was such a relief after having to hold him constantly. Since the woman was an expert on adoption, I went on to tell her about Daniel's background and how the drugs and alcohol in utero made him extra sensitive to touch. I also mentioned that his foster mom didn't touch him very much because it made him scream, and who wants to make a baby scream?

She looked quite serious, as if something was really wrong, and continued to ask me questions.

"Does he look back and check in with you when he crawls to touch something?" she wanted to know.

"Not really," I said.

"Does he turn to show you something new he's discovered?" she continued.

"No, not really. He's gotten very independent, and it's a lot easier this way," I replied.

After a few more questions and a few more answers, she finally said, "You folks are headed for trouble."

I had a sick feeling in the pit of my stomach. She went on to tell us that those symptoms indicated that Daniel wasn't appropriately attached to us, and because of what he'd been through, he might have an attachment deficit.

Attachment deficit? As in the reactive attachment disorder we'd seen in Angie? Pure panic set it.

"Don't worry," she said. "He's young enough that you can help him become securely attached fairly easily. You'll have to therapeutically parent him, though."

What in the world did that mean?

She went on to give us advice that would have sounded like psychobabble had we not seen attachment problems up close and personal.

She said that only John and I should hold Daniel, and that only I should feed him (not even John!). She told us that we should never let him hold his own bottle; he needed to depend on me to provide him with what he needed. He needed to be able to bond with and trust me. And then came the kicker: I needed to hold him and be face-to-face with him for almost eight hours a day!

My first thought was, *Are you kidding me?*

How in the world was I supposed to hold him for eight hours a day? We'd soon find out. We left the restaurant that day feeling unsettled and upset. In fact, I was gripped with fear and sick to my stomach. Were we headed for another repeat of Angie? One that would last eighteen years? It's hard to describe the dark cloud of dread that enveloped us. We prayed and reminded ourselves that Daniel was still young. We could fix this.

The truth is that God did a great thing for us that day. He reminded us through the Angie experience what happens to kids when they don't get the kind of start in life that *He* wants them to have.

The horror we lived through for a short time with Angie made us take this woman's words very seriously. Had we not gone through the Angie experience, we might not have listened to what she told us. It would have seemed like crazy advice that would only make our life harder in the short term.

Instead, by God's grace, we heeded her advice. It was hard, but it was doable. We did what she said. Honestly, we were scared not to. I finally discovered the miracle of the baby sling, so at least I had my arms. And after several months of this therapeutic parenting, we saw a difference. Daniel began to make good eye contact, and he was much healthier emotionally, more engaged, and more connected to us. He checked in with us if he was on a mission to do something. He shared his new-toy joy with us as he made new discoveries.

I still had to battle reasonable and unreasonable fears—reasonable fears that we'd not done enough to help Daniel become emotionally healthy, and unreasonable fears that at any moment he'd suddenly unattach from us. John and I alternated the roles of worrier and assurer, and back and forth we went, supporting each other through the fear along the way.

The time approached for Daniel's adoption to be finalized. We were beyond thrilled that the court would make final what we knew in our hearts: We were a forever family. As part of the normal process, we needed to schedule two more meetings with Veronica before adoption day—one at the Department of Human Services (DHS) and one at our home.

Foster parents don't have a lot of rights or privileges. But once the road is cleared for an adoption to be finalized, foster parents have quite a few more privileges, which include learning everything about the child they are about to adopt. So Veronica arranged a meeting with John and me at her DHS office so she could tell us things about Daniel's history that we didn't already know. She wanted to make sure we knew exactly what we were getting into and were fully committed. At this point, nothing would have changed our minds about adopting Daniel. This was simply a DHS formality from our perspective.

When we arrived at DHS on the day of the meeting, Veronica led us to a plain, small conference room with a round table and a few chairs. She told us to wait in the room while she went to get Daniel's file. Veronica returned a few minutes later carrying a stack of folders that completely filled her arms up to her chin and almost fell from her hands. *How in the world could a one-year-old have a file this big?* I wondered.

I wouldn't have to wait long for my answer. Veronica explained that Daniel's birth mother had also been in foster care. His maternal grandmother had been connected "to the system" and had received some government services. The file was big because it contained generations of sadness. Sad choices. Sad outcomes. Sad people. The whole thing was just so sad.

We learned that both Daniel's birth mother and birth father did drugs—marijuana and crystal methamphetamines, known as ice—and they had dropped out of high school. His birth father was known to child-welfare officials as a homeless street kid from a neighboring island who now lived in Waikiki on the streets.

Daniel's maternal uncle was a teenager and was in foster care. At the moment, however, he was missing after running away. Neither child-welfare officials nor his foster parents knew his whereabouts. Daniel's birth mother seemed to have disappeared; officials weren't able to contact her by phone or in person. They couldn't tell us any more about her current situation.

After that meeting, as John and I reflected on all the sadness in this family, we were grateful that God was going to break the generational cycle for our son, and we resolved to do everything in our power to help.

Veronica came to our house for our final meeting before the big court day. As she walked to the kitchen table to set out the last bit of paperwork we needed to complete, she bluntly told us a rather weighty piece of news: Daniel had a great-aunt on the Big Island.

John and I stopped dead in our tracks.

"She wants to adopt Daniel," Veronica continued, never changing her inflection.

It was as if I'd been kicked in the stomach. I couldn't breathe. I grabbed my stomach and gasped. John was just frozen.

"But we talked through it," Veronica continued. "She's a foster parent too, and she understands how awful it would be if someone took her little one from her. She doesn't want to hurt Daniel by taking him away from y'all, since he's settled and secure. She was glad he's in a good home and has a good future in front of him."

We wanted to give Veronica the biggest hug in the world. Just like that, as quickly as the fear had come, it was gone. Veronica had done her job well by trying to effectuate what she believed was in Daniel's best interest. Of course, a judge had to concur, but the recommendations of DHS would hold significant sway in the process. With relief, we signed the papers so that Daniel's adoption could be finalized.

When adoption day came, the joy was overwhelming. We arrived at the courthouse early, all dressed up.

Family court is an extremely dark and depressing place, filled with brokenness and despair. Divorce, child custody, child support, child abuse, domestic violence, and termination of parental rights are daily staples. Adoption finalizations are a ray of light in this dark place, and everyone from the security guards to the court clerks and judges are usually happy to participate in this life-changing event. But we had a no-nonsense judge who walked us through the legal recitals and requirements and eventually banged her gavel declaring the adoption final.

The date was March 13, 2001. Just eleven days after Daniel's first birthday.

It was over. The relief was hard to describe. We were now a family—officially. And we were a happy one! We loved being with Daniel as much as we could. We were amazed at how much we loved him, and like all first-time parents, we wondered how we could ever love another child as much as we loved him.

We didn't worry about it, though. We were very much enjoying the gift of parenting, but we were in no hurry for more children. Later that day we went to a professional photographer for our first family portrait. What a blessing!

9

Fifteen Minutes

T hings were going well with Daniel, and after the adoption was finalized, we began to settle into a very nice routine. About that time, an intriguing opportunity presented itself. As director of Hawaii Family Forum, I was a frequent guest on both Christian radio and talk radio. One day the manager of a local radio station took me to lunch and proposed that I host a new afternoon drive-time show. The station was well known, featuring some of the most popular national talk-radio shows.

This new endeavor would take quite a bit of time, so I reduced my workload with HFF to ensure that these activities wouldn't interfere with my family responsibilities. Daniel was my priority, and I wasn't about to let anything jeopardize that. I had already been working less than full-time from my home office, but now I would do even less direct work for HFF and just see how it went. The HFF board of directors was always so gracious and accommodating.

John was incredibly supportive as well. This was a pretty big deal. It seemed like an opportunity I couldn't refuse. I thought of all the good I could accomplish by helping to develop the afternoon drive-time market in Hawaii and mobilize thousands of people to get involved in family issues.

I was moving full steam ahead with this new venture, and the inaugural day of the show was quickly approaching. I was getting really nervous, but I had all my first-show guests lined up, including Hawaii's state senate president.

Between the time I was offered the talk show and the first day we were going live, our country experienced the terrible tragedy of 9/11. Like the rest of the nation, everyone in Hawaii grieved the loss of life and the devastating impact of terror on the families and the country.

One of the consequences of the attacks was an economic decline. Commerce, along with so many other aspects of our national life, was adversely affected.

The morning of my first show, I was filled with excitement as I got ready for the day. Then the phone rang. It was the local station manager. I figured he was calling to encourage me on my big first day. Instead, he dropped a bomb. He told me that my new show, along with all other new endeavors, had been canceled by his higher-ups on the U.S. mainland.

I thought he was joking.

He wasn't. He went on, in all seriousness, to explain that in the aftermath of 9/11, corporate executives were pulling back on anything new.

But the senate president was scheduled to come on the show in just a few hours! That was no small thing. And I had significantly modified my future plans for the Hawaii Family Forum. I had rearranged my entire life to get ready for this show!

And it was all gone in one phone call.

I was incredulous and somewhat panicky. John and I had relied on this opportunity financially and in many other ways. Why had this happened? Why had the Lord allowed us to rearrange our lives for an opportunity He knew would fall through? We set about trying to undo the changes we had made to our schedules and other parts of our lives to accommodate that opportunity.

I was disappointed and confused.

What was the Lord up to?

In the weeks that followed, as John and I prayed and contemplated our future, a thought kept coming to my mind: *I should call the social worker; there's a great need.* I knew that other kids in Hawaii needed families, but John and I really weren't thinking too much about adopting more children at that point. We assumed we'd likely adopt again, but we were very happy with Daniel and content with our lives. We were also enjoying the calm and peace we were experiencing after so much turmoil.

But the words "call the social worker; there's a great need" kept echoing in my mind for several days. And since I'm a little slow about these things, it took awhile before it dawned on me that the Lord was impressing this on my heart, and I had better pay attention.

I told John about it, and he said, "Well, call her."

We weren't thinking or feeling strongly either way. But I couldn't get this thought out of my head. I wanted to be obedient to whatever God was leading me to do, so I called Veronica even though I had no clue why. I told her that John and I weren't really looking to adopt again at that time, but I knew there was a great need, and I wanted her to call us if she thought we could help.

She said, "Okay," and that was it. I wondered why I had felt so compelled to call her, but having done so, I quickly moved on. It was October 24, 2001.

The day after I made that call, I had an HFF board meeting to adjust our organizational plans following the radio show cancellation. Then I headed home after a productive but busy day. At about eight o'clock that evening, John and I were snuggled on the couch, sharing the details of our day. Daniel was sleeping upstairs.

The phone rang. It was Veronica. In her typically flat but accented voice, she said, "Kelly, remember when you said to call you if I had a need?"

I replied, "Yeah, Veronica, what's up? How can we help?"

With the emotion of someone reading the phone book and with no warm-up, she simply said, "A baby girl was born at 4:00 a.m. on the streets of Waikiki to a schizophrenic homeless woman—do you want her?"

WHAT?

I began to ask Veronica a million questions. "What do you know about the mom? What about the dad? What do you think the future will bring? Will she need an adoptive family? Is there anyone else who will want her?" She patiently answered my questions as best she could with limited information. The baby seemed healthy enough after birth, her mom was Vietnamese, and there was no information about the birth father.

The bottom line was that this baby needed to leave the hospital soon and be placed in a home. Beyond that, Veronica couldn't assure us of anything else.

Wow.

It was slowly dawning on me why the Lord had laid it on my heart to make that phone call. John was quick to recognize the Lord's leading. According to him, this was an easy call. God was in this. God had brought us to this moment. That was about the only thing we were sure of at that moment. But what more did we need when that piece was so clear? After all, that's the only part that really matters in the end.

After rattling off all the details to John, I asked Veronica a very reasonable question—or so I thought.

"Can we pray and call you in the morning?" I asked.

"You've got fifteen minutes," she responded.

Fifteen minutes. Oh my goodness. I hung up. John and I prayed. We called her right back. Of course we would help.

We would go to the hospital the next day and pick up this little girl. She needed a name (her birth mother was too ill to give her one), and we chose Anna Grace. It was a biblical name from the second chapter of Luke. In the Bible, Anna fasted and prayed and worshipped God in the temple day and night.

God deals with us in such funny ways, doesn't He? One moment life is going along a certain way; the next moment a phone call changes everything.

I was so nervous. I'd never parented a newborn. In fact, I was terrified of newborns. To me, they were just so fragile and otherworldly, and one wrong move could kill them. Daniel was almost six months old when he came home, past the terrifying stage to this naive and inexperienced mother.

I didn't sleep one second that whole night. Not one second. Thankfully, John slept. He was excited but much more calm than I was. At this point, Daniel was only one and a half years old, but we told him what was going on first thing in the morning. Not that he could fully understand, but things were about to get exciting. We had only twenty-four hours to get ready!

The night before, I had called my dear friend and neighbor Dana, who was a nurse and had a daughter Daniel's age. When we told her what was happening, she declared an all-hands-on-deck situation and offered to help us with meals and shopping and whatever else we needed. She went to the store and got us newborn diapers, formula, a car seat, and anything else she thought we might need.

We also called my dad and his wife and their two children, my sister and brother (ages eleven and thirteen), who had moved to Hawaii to be close to us and because my dad loved the warm weather. They had come for a visit Christmas of 1999 and simply never returned to Wisconsin. Hawaii was in desperate need of special-education teachers, so my dad and his wife had been able to find jobs rather easily. My dad had gone back to Wisconsin alone, packed up and sold their house, and returned to the island. They had been renting a house within walking distance of us.

When I told them the news, they sprang into action as well, helping us get ready for baby Anna's homecoming the following day. Having the emotional support, the practical help, and the presence of family and friends made all the difference to us.

The morning of October 26 arrived, and it was time to go to the hospital to pick up our daughter. John and I sensed from the information Veronica had supplied that Anna would be staying with us for good, but we didn't have any idea what the future held. We would be Anna's foster parents, who were willing to adopt her, and she'd be with us for as long as God determined. We didn't know anything other than that—and the fact that God had clearly and dramatically brought us to this point.

In addition to the other factors that were making us very nervous, John and I were concerned about the possibility of running into Anna's birth mother at the hospital. We had been told she was unstable and that security had been called in and would be there when we picked up Anna.

By the time we arrived at the hospital, Anna's birth mother had just walked out, never to return, but we didn't know that. We had prayed for her, and our hearts broke for her plight. We were thankful, however, that her baby was safe. Life on the streets for a newborn with a schizophrenic mother would likely have ended very, very badly. The thought sent shivers down my spine.

We went to the floor of the hospital where all the teeny babies were cared for. Daniel was wonderfully behaved and excited. As a member of the hospital staff was giving us directions, a nurse wheeled a baby past us on a cart. There she was! It was Anna! She was absolutely tiny with plenty of jet-black hair and almond eyes that were barely visible. We were so excited.

The nurses showed us how to clean the umbilical-cord area, which completely grossed me out. I'm probably one of the most squeamish people on earth. The nurses also briefed us on how to make Anna's bottles and when to feed her. It was as if I had landed on another planet; the whole thing was so foreign to me. My mom didn't live on the islands, so she wasn't there to show me what to do. John had no clue.

All the way home, I was worried that Anna would start crying and I wouldn't know what to do. Mercifully, she slept. We got home and took homecoming pictures, just as we had done with Daniel. Our family and neighborhood friends came to greet our new little peanut. It was such a joyous time. She was so calm and quiet, content and sleepy. I was grateful.

That night I was exhausted. No sleep the night before had me on edge. Anna was in a basinet beside my bed, and I was terrified she would stop breathing in the night. At about eleven o'clock, she started to cry. I panicked. She cried even more. I started to cry. John was asleep while I was going through this, because he had to get up at 5:00 a.m. to commute to Honolulu.

This is hilarious in retrospect, but it wasn't at the time. I rocked Anna; she cried harder. I was getting tense, which didn't help. Finally, at that late hour, I called Dana, sobbing as I explained to her that I couldn't get Anna to stop crying.

"Did you give her a bottle?" she asked calmly.

"Okay, I'll try that," I whimpered back, never wondering why I hadn't thought of that rather obvious suggestion.

Anna took the bottle and fell sound asleep for almost three hours. I, however, didn't sleep a wink for a second night in a row. Thus began the typical sleep-deprived struggle every parent around the world experiences who has two kids under the age of two.

Notwithstanding the sleep deprivation, which just about did me in, John and I were shell-shocked by what God had done in one twenty-four-hour period. He had changed our lives forever—again.

Shortly thereafter we received a congratulatory note from our senior pastor celebrating the fact that we now had two *keiki*. *Keiki* is Hawaiian for children, and it remains one of our favorite words.

Things continued in pretty typical fashion for about a year. That first Christmas with our two *keiki* was one of my favorites of all time. At this point, we were just waiting for the formalities of the legal process to catch up with what we knew in our hearts: We were now a family of four, and we all loved our new baby girl so much. Daniel was so gentle with her, and John and I were crazy about her.

The bliss that characterized that first year with Anna, however, was shattered by yet another phone call from a social worker—a call that devastated our lives and plunged us into one of our darkest hours.

10

Our Darkest Hour

After Anna's birth mother walked out of the hospital, child-welfare officials never saw her again, and no one had any idea who Anna's birth father was. We were just waiting for the legal system to finalize her adoption. Nothing seemed to be stopping us. The social workers and guardian ad litem favored us adopting Anna. It seemed like a picture-perfect story with a happy ending.

We were the only family Anna had ever known. She was happy and healthy and loved, with a great future ahead of her. Since the birth father was unknown, we didn't have to worry about terminating his rights. And since no one could find the birth mother, the paperwork couldn't be served. When that happens, in order to ensure due process, a notice is placed in the newspaper in a final effort to locate the parents.

As all this was proceeding, we were the happiest little family of four one could imagine. Eleven months had passed since Anna had come home with us. Then one afternoon, the phone rang.

"Hi, Kelly; it's Joan."

I figured Joan, Anna's social worker, was just checking in. I'll never forget her next bone-chilling words: "Kelly, I know you love Anna, *but* . . ."

I felt as though I'd been kicked in the stomach, and I let out the longest, loudest, most guttural gasp. I went into panic mode, knowing something was terribly wrong. There were no "buts" to our future with Anna.

You see, Joan was calling to tell us that our worst nightmare was going to become a reality. Anna's birth mother, Louise, had been found. And although she was still mentally ill and unable to care for Anna, she had identified relatives on the U.S. mainland, and they wanted Anna.

It took some time to sink in. They wanted our daughter. This was an unthinkable horror. Life without Anna wasn't something I wanted to endure. I just kept thinking, *We can't live without our baby girl.* We were all incredibly bonded and in love—any family with little ones knows the feeling.

I want to pause at this point and note that many people can't quite grasp the gravity of what I'm describing. One response we often hear is "She's not your 'real' child, and after all, the people who wanted her are her blood relatives."

To those of you who are parents, the only way I can explain it is this: Think back to the time when you gave birth to your baby, who is now one year old. Remember what that was like? Well, it was and is no different for John and me. We couldn't love Anna any more had she been born from my tummy rather than my heart. Now imagine receiving a phone call out of the blue announcing that someone would be taking your baby away. Just pause and think through that. That's the horror that was confronting us.

After my guttural gasp, I grilled the social worker with questions and then called John to recount the conversation.

"Can you talk? I need you to sit down," I said.

"What's wrong?" he asked instantly.

"The social worker called. There have been some developments in Anna's case. Her birth mother got picked up by the police for trying to pass counterfeit money. It's a federal offense, so the feds have sent her to a mainland facility to get her well enough to stand trial."

This was the official legal reason the feds were holding her pretrial, but we were told, and because of my legal training I suspected, they were just trying to help her. She was being held under the legal pretense of getting her well enough to stand trial, but they weren't going to prosecute her. She was intensely mentally ill, and there was no other way to get her the help she needed.

"What?" John said, incredulous.

I told him that since Anna's birth mother had been on medication for some time by this point, she had become more lucid and had identified relatives on the U.S. mainland. Prison officials had contacted the relatives, who had then called child-welfare officials. Apparently, the birth mother's relatives were professionals and seemed to have good lives on the mainland. They had been through years of trouble with Anna's birth mother. They had tried to help her repeatedly, but she was always inconsistent in taking her medication. When she was off her meds, she would become very ill and live on the streets.

The birth mother's relatives hadn't known about Anna, but now that they did, they wanted her. I could tell that John was stunned and scared, just like I was. I found out later that after we hung up, he went to a private area at his workplace and wept.

"Okay, here's the deal," I continued. "The social worker seemed to be calling to tell me that the state would recommend Anna go live with the relatives. But by the end of our conversation, she backed way off and just left me with the reality that the process will need to work itself out and that none of us, including her, can have any idea at this point how things will turn out.

"But there is some good news. Once they terminate parental rights, the case will go to a different social worker who will then exercise due diligence and recommend the best placement for Anna. And guess who the social worker will be?" I said, trying to impart hope to my husband.

"Who?" John asked.

"Veronica," I stated confidently.

John was as relieved as I was that Veronica would be the one in control of Anna's (and our) future. And though the specifics are a bit blurry to me now, I recall trying to remain calm and confident. While the judge would ultimately make the decision, Veronica's recommendation was the key factor, and even though she had to investigate what would be in Anna's best interest, we couldn't do any better than Veronica as our social worker.

We knew one thing: We would fight for Anna with everything we had. We weren't going to lose our daughter.

Let the advocacy begin.

I called Veronica and began my major lobbying effort. Thankfully, I think she was fond of us and felt pretty invested in our little family, which she had helped create.

"She's healthy and completely bonded to us," I launched in. "We're her parents, and Daniel is her brother. Her birth relatives can still be aunties, uncles, and grandparents, but *we are her mom and dad.*"

Veronica was calm and professional, but she did give me that glimmer of hope I was looking for. The birth relatives would have a lot of work to do to even be considered as adoptive parents for Anna. Veronica would talk with them and tell them about us.

She also suggested that we write them a letter, which we did.

Talk about pressure. The letter began something like this: "We're sure you are as surprised to learn about us as we were to learn about you. We wanted to write and send pictures right away because we want you to know how well Anna is doing . . ."

I went on to tell them all about Anna's wonderful life (subtext: Please don't ruin our lives by ripping our baby girl away from all she knows), complete with lots of details and pictures showing the close relationship between Anna and Daniel.

I also told them that we would always keep them posted on how Anna was doing. They could be her aunt, uncle, cousins, and so forth, in her life. We could make this work. Please let the adoption proceed.

John and I read it over and over, and finally, after much prayer and agony, we sent the letter to them via Veronica. Now we would wait and pray.

While we were waiting, we contacted a lawyer who would help us fight to the end for Anna. We would do everything in our power to keep our daughter. We alerted everyone we knew who had money and told them that we might need to borrow some to wage a legal battle for Anna. My next call was to the guardian ad litem. I needed her on our side. She needed to fight for Anna to stay with the only family she knew. The guardian said she was with us. We'd all just need to walk through the process and see what happened.

I began to keep close tabs on what was happening with Anna's birth mother. Because she was a federal prisoner, a website was available for us to find out her whereabouts and status. For the longest time, she was in a mainland prison. I logged on constantly, even though I knew it was pointless. Something about seeing her status made me feel as though I had some control. It was completely ridiculous, but I did it anyway.

Spiritually, John and I were going through an emotional hell. I cried constantly. John and I prayed day and night. We fought hard to trust God. Sometimes we did; sometimes we didn't. In some ways, I feel that I failed this test miserably. God really did give me peace. But for reasons I'm not entirely sure about, I didn't always walk in it. I fretted and cried and agonized. I wish that I had held to the peace that was available to me, but all I can do is share the truth with you. I struggled to trust God. I was afraid. It wasn't easy for John either. We would take turns falling apart and keeping the faith.

I remember literally screaming out to God once while I was taking a shower, "Okay, You win! I will trust You whatever that means, even if my worst fears come true." For me, it was always a moment-by-moment choice to either walk in God's peace or give in to my worst, raw fear. It was a day-by-day battle.

I know that lots of marriages suffer real blows during difficult times like this, but thankfully, even in the darkest times, John and I clung to each other. When we were hurting or afraid, we'd turn to each other rather than against each other. We also had a very supportive, wonderful church family who prayed for us, which was a great blessing. And our families in Hawaii and on the U.S. mainland were all very supportive. Deeanna, especially, was a shoulder for me to cry on.

John also took comfort in my passionate lobbying for our family and my thorough process work. I reported every detail to him, and we discussed every aspect over and over. We covered all our bases as best we could. I would badger both Veronica and the guardian ad litem for information as often as I could. One time I even called the birth mother's lawyer, who couldn't really talk to me. At some point, my neurotic website checks revealed that Louise had left the federal prison on the mainland. I learned that she had improved enough to be transferred to a mental-health placement facility in Hawaii. As I suspected, no charges would be filed against her even though she was apparently somewhat lucid.

John and I really wanted to connect with Louise, though that prospect frightened us. There was something unsettling about the thought of meeting either of my children's birth mothers. To be honest, I felt somewhat threatened. But John and I had a love and compassion for Anna's birth mother. She had chosen life for Anna, and we would always be grateful to her for that. We also wanted her to have the peace of knowing that Anna was doing great—beyond great. She was the happiest, healthiest, most-loved baby in the world.

But by the time we found out where Louise was located, she had just walked out of the facility—again. She couldn't be held against her will because she wasn't a danger to herself or others. No one knew where she was.

John and I tried to find her. We even walked the streets of Waikiki, searching for her and asking homeless folks if they knew her. Several times we met people who knew her, and they'd suggest looking here or there. My heart would beat wildly because I thought we might be close.

Once, we even approached a woman we thought might be Louise. The woman was scared and wild-eyed, cowering with a shopping cart full of stuff. She didn't appear to speak English. It wasn't Anna's birth mother. Our hearts sank.

I formed a relationship with the folks at the local mental-health/ homeless-outreach organization. They knew Louise and occasionally saw her. I gave them a note and a picture of Anna to give her if they ever saw her. We wanted her to have a measure of peace if that was possible.

This organization was just a few blocks from where I parked when I went to the state capitol to lobby, so I would occasionally drop in to see if there was any news. We couldn't find Louise, despite our best efforts. But we had other things to worry about. We had a potential legal battle to wage and win. No one—and we meant *no one*—was taking our Anna Grace away from us.

11

Answered Prayers

Months went by, and we hadn't received a response from Anna's relatives to the letter we'd written. Months. Can you believe that? It felt like years to us. It was a torturous wait.

It seemed as if our very lives hung in the balance.

As we waited, it was as though a dark cloud enveloped every aspect of our lives. Everything we did as a happy family of four was marred by the fear lurking in our hearts and minds: Would this be the last time we would enjoy this activity as a family?

The Bible says the Enemy comes to steal, kill, and destroy (John 10:10). He was stealing our joy, killing our peace, and destroying our dreams for the future.

Our first Christmas with our two children had been one of the best ever, but the next Christmas was one of the worst. I kept wondering, *Will we get to have future Christmases?* My family visited from the mainland, and I worried whether Anna would get to grow up knowing her cousins, her auntie, and her grandma.

I cried a lot that Christmas. John is less emotional than I am, but this was an excruciating time for him, too. All we could do was wait and keep talking to each other, praying, and trusting God.

Other aspects of our future were now weighing heavily on us as well. John was about to retire from the air force, and we didn't know what he would do or whether we'd need to return to the U.S. mainland. Hawaii's cost of living is among the highest in the nation, and we just didn't know how we'd continue to make ends meet there. But we sure couldn't go anywhere until the situation with Anna was resolved.

⤜⤛

Months continued to go by. One Saturday—March 29, 2003, to be exact—the sun was shining outside, but our hearts were heavy and dark as we took the kids to the Honolulu Zoo. It was all I could do not to fall apart publicly, wondering if we'd ever do this again with Anna. It had been such a long wait. By this point, we'd almost resigned ourselves to the belief that answers weren't coming anytime soon. We could only hope that the longer she remained with us, the less likely it would be that the authorities would take her away from us.

We returned home from the zoo that day to find a voice mail waiting for me. I quickly recognized the voice.

"John, it's Veronica," I whispered urgently. And in that beautiful Southern accent, our social worker said with a shaky voice full of emotion, "Your prayers have been answered; you will be able to adopt Anna." She explained that she'd finally gotten a call from Anna's birth relatives, and based on our letter, they really didn't want to traumatize Anna by taking her away from us, so they would consent to the adoption.

I shrieked and started crying again—this time for joy. Joy and relief like I'd never known. John and I hugged. He cried, too. Then we loudly exclaimed our thanks to God.

The kids were a bit alarmed, and Daniel wanted to know why we were crying. We explained that sometimes grown-ups cry for happiness. That was all the explanation he needed. They had known nothing about what was going on, other than what they could sense from the grief of their parents, who were trying hard to pretend everything was okay.

Anna's adoption was finalized, and another glorious day at the courthouse left us happy, tired, and looking to the future.

12

Back and Forth

Through a series of events, including my grandparents' failing health, we felt the Lord calling us to do something I'd have bet a million dollars I'd never do: move back to my little hometown of Wisconsin Dells. It's expensive moving to and from Hawaii, and we decided that for financial reasons, we needed to make the move in conjunction with John's retirement in just a few months.

With Anna's adoption finalized, we were through one adrenaline rush and on to the next one: moving across the globe. Leaving our church family and the Hawaii Family Forum was incredibly sad, but we were ready for the change the Lord seemed to be bringing our way.

So we went back to the U.S. mainland, to the heart of the Midwest. Our plan was to live a simple life. We wanted to work as little as possible and enjoy as much time as we could with our kids. I would also get to spend invaluable time caring for my ailing grandparents at the end of their lives.

One might think we were crazy to leave Honolulu to go back to Wisconsin, but we were very happy. We felt we'd followed God's leading, and so we put down roots in my hometown.

We had a great time reconnecting with our relatives, who were much easier to see when we weren't living across the Pacific Ocean. And along with my wonderful aunt and uncle, we helped plant an evangelical church in our little town. I did some contract lobbying in Madison part-time while John was home with the kids full-time for the first time. I was home quite a bit too.

We also spent lots of time caring for my grandparents. My grandfather received a terminal cancer diagnosis just a few weeks after we arrived, and he was gone within five months. Helping care for him right to his last breath was one of the greatest honors of my life. I loved him very much and was able to demonstrate that love to him right up to the end. After his death, I became very active caring for my grandmother, including regularly showering and shaving her. That may sound like a pain, and sometimes it was, but it was a great joy, too. My grandma and I giggled a lot, and to this day, I smile thinking about those times.

I also had the great honor of leading my cousin to Christ. She in turn led most of her family to Christ, and they are now active in the church we helped plant—more things that still make me smile. The kids were doing great, and we loved introducing them to snow for the first time. We had fun doing winter activities and enjoying the fireplace on cold days.

During this time, Daniel, who was now three, began to blink his eyes repeatedly. He would blink more times than we could possibly count. I would tell him to stop it, but it went on incessantly. It seemed so odd to us.

We took him to a doctor who, with all the bedside manner of a bedpan, handed us a piece of paper and told us that Daniel had Tourette's syndrome and that his eye blinking was a form of tics.

Our son has Tourette's syndrome? Please tell me you're kidding.

I felt sick with worry. Fear came over me again. The doctor told us that at this stage there was nothing to do but ignore it and tell everyone involved in his life to ignore it as well. There was no telling whether it would get worse or better.

I clearly remember praying and crying out to God about Daniel. As I did, God impressed something on my heart and mind in a way I've rarely felt Him do before or since. I felt Him remind me that my prayer for my children should always be for their spiritual health above everything else. It was as though God asked me how I knew He wasn't going to use this very thing—Tourette's syndrome—to strengthen Daniel spiritually.

Wow! I felt such peace in my heart with that realization. It made such a difference. I shared all this with John. Though I was greatly encouraged, John struggled a bit longer. He felt a lot of anger toward Daniel's birth parents for their irresponsible choices that contributed to his physical difficulties. It took more time for forgiveness to take place in his heart. But he got there.

Over the years, Daniel's Tourette's syndrome, or tics as we call them in our family, have gone through periods of getting better and then getting worse. He's undergone a therapy called neurofeedback now for several years. As I write this, Daniel is eleven years old, and the tics are acting up again. Just days ago, he told me that for the first time, kids at school noticed the tics and made fun of him. I wanted to march straight up to the school and take on those kids, but Daniel seemed okay. He also told me that one of his friends had stood up for him. That made him happy.

John and I talk a lot with Daniel about trusting and walking with God. I remember the reminder God gave me way back when

Daniel was first diagnosed, and I believe that He has great plans for Daniel's life. Recently, out of the clear blue, Daniel handed me something he'd written at church:

God means everything to me. He means everything to me because He made me. He heals me, and He died on the cross for me, and He gave me a home with a family. He didn't just give to me, He gave everything to me, including His life.

Again I'm reminded that God is so faithful.

Even while we were in Wisconsin, we stayed in close touch with all our Hawaii friends, and I stayed in almost daily contact with the folks at the Hawaii Family Forum. They needed help, and it was never just a job for me. After a year in Wisconsin Dells, John and I began to wonder what might be next. My grandpa had passed away, my grandma was settled, and we were beginning to sense the restlessness we'd experience whenever the Lord was about to move us.

Truth be told, we were happy in Wisconsin Dells. We knew God had brought us here. But we just didn't feel it was where we belonged for the long haul. For one thing, our kids were Asian and Pacific Islander, and my Wisconsin hometown wasn't even remotely diverse. We worried about that. We'd also wanted to send our children to a Christian school, but there wasn't one nearby. We didn't know what the future held for us, but we were starting to feel unsettled.

During that time, several of the HFF board members had been talking to me about what seemed like the *crazy* proposition of our moving back to Hawaii. Move back to Hawaii? Really? Move back over the ocean? Our friends and families probably thought we were nuts, but it seemed this was where God was leading us, and we were open to it.

"Who even thinks like this?" John and I would say to each other.

But in relatively short order, the HFF board had agreed to pay our way back, and John had been offered a job at our former home church in Kaimuki. His job meant that our kids could go to our church's Christian school for free. The Kaimuki Christian Church was even going to let us rent one of the homes on the church property.

It was perfect. So we moved back to Hawaii. John enjoyed his job. I loved being back at the Hawaii Family Forum. Our church family and friends were so happy to have us back. We were home. And it's where we planned to be forever.

13

African Faces

One of the many great things about the Kaimuki Christian Church was its heart for missions, outreach, and orphans. Through our involvement with outreach there, John and I had connected with a man named Mike who was originally from Kenya and had been orphaned as a teen. He'd been adopted by American missionaries and had come to the United States, eventually getting his master's degree at a Christian university. He had a great life in America, but he felt compelled to go back to Kenya and help his hurting people by bringing them the good news of Christ and physical comfort as well.

Our church partnered with Mike to build a school and orphanage in Kenya. To better inform our church about what he was doing in Kenya, Mike visited our congregation. One Sunday in November of 2005, Mike was preaching and showing us pictures of children from his homeland who desperately, and I mean desperately, needed our help.

On the big screen was a seemingly endless sea of faces of children—all orphans—all longing for families, for food, and for a good life. As I heard his message and saw the photos, I started to cry.

Now, I know it probably seems like I cry a lot, but I'm not typi-cally that way! I'm actually a very upbeat person. Bubbly even.

But what was happening inside of me on this beautiful Hono-lulu Sunday morning expressed itself in deep, gut-wrenching sobs. *Oh my goodness*, I thought, *how embarrassing*. I was sitting in church, toward the front, and I was actually making noise from crying so hard. People were starting to look.

My nose was running. My shoulders were shaking. I tried bit-ing my tongue really hard to make myself stop crying, but nothing worked.

My heart ached for those poor kids. They were all alone. They needed families. There were many families all around me in church that morning. I kept thinking, *The church really needs to do some-thing. We can't just claim to be followers of Jesus and do nothing!*

And then the personal conversation in my head began. It went like this:

My heart is broken for these kids. We should do something.

But I don't want any more kids.

Really, Kelly? Really? You have two kids. Two. Two isn't very many kids. God has blessed your socks off, and you don't think you have any more room for even one more kid? That's ridiculous, I said to myself.

I found out later that John was having a similar conversation in his head. That's one of the ways we've come to know that the Lord is orchestrating the conversation.

So we had lots and lots of conversation and prayer about this topic. We really didn't want any more kids. Our adoption experi-ences to date had been harrowing, and we just wanted to settle down and be a nice normal family of four. But then again, how could we not be willing to get involved? I couldn't get those African faces out of my mind.

December 1997—
John and Kelly, pre-kids,
Manoa, Oahu, Hawaii

September 9, 2000—
Daniel's Homecoming Day,
Ewa Beach, Oahu, Hawaii

March 13, 2001—
Daniel's Adoption Day

March 13, 2001—
Daniel's Adoption Day,
Honolulu Courthouse

October 26, 2001-
Anna's homecoming day,
Ewa Beach, Oahu, Hawaii

October 2001-
Kelly and Anna

Christmas 2001-
Ko Olina,
West Oahu, Hawaii

2003- Daniel and Deeanna,
Oahu, Hawaii

'03 4 25

Christmas 2003-
Daniel and Anna,
Wisconsin Dells, Wisconsin

Christmas 2004-
Daniel and Anna,
Kaimuki, Oahu, Hawaii

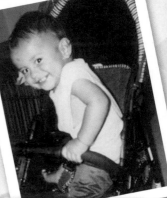

circa 2003–
Joshua, before
he came to us

2004– Anna enjoying the breeze,
Kaimuki, Oahu, Hawaii

December 12, 2006– Joshua's adoption day, Honolulu, Hawaii

2007- Before Hope's adoption, Manoa, Oahu, Hawaii

November 17, 2007- Hope's adoption day,
Honolulu, Hawaii

2007- Hope's first day of preschool, Manoa, Oahu, Hawaii

November 2007- National Adoption Month Celebration, Governor's Conference Room, Honolulu State Capitol

2011- Hope (top), Joshua (right),
Anna and Hope (bottom),
Colorado Springs, Colorado

2011- The Rosati Family

"What is God calling us to do?" John would ask. "What is our comfort compared to a life of desperation and loneliness?" he probed.

"Let's just pray about it," I would answer.

We had many concerns, all of which could be rationalized as wise and sound: *We already have two kids. Will we be able to give them enough attention and care? How will we afford more kids? Life with Daniel and Anna is great, so why would we want to risk going through that difficult process again?*

Those were and are all reasonable concerns. At the end of the day, however, none seemed insurmountable in light of the need, or more important, in light of our continued sense of God's leading. I would come to the conclusion "no way" in my mind but not have any peace.

The bottom line was that God had blessed us so much, and we knew that His heart was beating for these orphan children. All our reasons not to proceed were part selfish, part risk averse, part faithless—even though they all seemed reasonable. Please don't misunderstand, John and I feel strongly that this is what happened with *us*. It was our personal experience. Not everyone is called to adopt. The Bible makes it clear that we are all called to care for orphans in some way (James 1:27), but we believe that no one should ever pursue adoption without a clear leading from the Lord.

We sought counsel from godly friends, but the advice we received was mixed. Many people thought we'd done enough and really should just help others get involved at this point. But plenty of people encouraged us to adopt again. In the end, John and I felt in our hearts that the Lord was telling us to do both: Get others involved *and* open the circle of our family and welcome in another child.

To be honest, John was more open and excited than I was at that moment. I felt that my hands were full already.

We talked to Daniel and Anna, of course, who were quite clear from the get-go. "What? There are kids who don't have families?" they'd say in total horror. "Well, we have a family. They can come live with us." They were five and four at the time.

Daniel's and Anna's open and willing attitudes at such young ages helped us cut through the clutter in our own minds. One night we had been looking at African orphanage websites on the computer and the pictures of beautiful little children on the screen. I had apparently left the computer on overnight, and when I came into the room the next morning, I saw Daniel (he didn't know I was awake yet) touching the face of a child on the screen and talking to her, saying, "Don't worry! We'll come for you. We're coming."

Can you imagine the feeling that would give you? That image will be seared into my mind forever. I wanted to cry. I felt happy and proud of Daniel's beautiful heart. I also felt convicted. My little son seemed to see all this so clearly, with God's heart. Me, not so much.

Another time both Anna and Daniel started yelling for us to come quickly. I thought they were having some big fight over a toy or some other nonsense. Instead, they were watching one of those Sally Struthers' ads on TV about kids in desperate poverty. Daniel and Anna were aghast. They were adamant that we had to do something about this and help those kids.

God so often speaks to us through our children.

John was excited and clear that we needed to do this. His heart was really ready before mine was. My final position was this: Out of gratitude and obedience to God, we would do this. We would adopt from Africa.

14

It Was Only
a Test

S o we swung into action pursuing adoption from Africa, but
something interesting happened. Despite what we thought
was a great local connection in Mike, every door we tried to
open got shut tightly in our faces.

Our e-mails went unanswered, and phone calls weren't returned.
We were told we'd have to live in Kenya for six months, which wasn't
something we could do. Our key contacts all of a sudden became
unavailable.

What was going on?

We didn't know, but clearly this adopting from Africa thing
wasn't lifting off the ground.

"What's up with that, Lord?" John and I both questioned. "We
thought we'd sensed Your leading very clearly. What was that whole
process we just went through about, if not this?"

I knew one thing: I was relieved.

Not so for John, Daniel, and Anna. They were disappointed.
One night after a long talk about what we should do, John and I
were reminded of the strategy that served us well from the start in

this adoption journey: *Let's simply be available to God and just see what happens.*

So without thinking too much about it, I set out to schedule all our appointments, get our physicals, update our home study, and so on. Thankfully, we didn't have to retake the training classes, since we'd adopted fairly recently.

When the day came to have our fingerprints taken, John and I stole away from our jobs and had a date at the fingerprint place. Afterward, we sat outside in gorgeous downtown Honolulu and enjoyed each other's company over lunch. We relished having a few minutes away from the demands of work and kids to enjoy some peace and alone time.

The fingerprints were it. They were the last step in getting ready. Now we would wait.

Turns out we didn't have to wait too long.

That very night—you guessed it—the phone rang. It was dear Deeanna Wallace, and she said in her sweet voice, "Kelly, remember when you said you wanted to adopt a toddler?"

In my mind, I thought, *Um, yes. That was like five years ago when we first started this. That was before we had two kids.*

"Yes?" I replied cautiously.

"Well," she said, "I just got a call about a little boy in foster care who needs an adoptive family."

I felt a knot in my stomach. I thought this was just a test. *Not yet*, my mind was protesting. But God's timing was as clear as anything could be in my heart.

"What's his story?" I asked.

"His name is Joshua. He's almost four, and well, he doesn't really talk. And he's not potty trained. Oh, and he might have a mental disability; they're not sure."

I also learned that Joshua had been born to an immigrant mother from Micronesia, who didn't speak much English. She had married an American man, but drugs, alcohol, and homelessness were the hallmarks of their lives together for the first years of Joshua's young life.

One day his mother took him to the babysitter and never returned to pick him up. She just never came back. It hurts my heart to even think about this. The sitter called child-welfare officials, and Joshua was put in foster care. He was in an emergency shelter home, and then he was moved to his second foster home. But he was only there a few weeks because he cried constantly and the family couldn't stand it. He was deeply grieving, no doubt.

His next foster home turned out to be abusive. So he was moved to another foster home, where he was currently staying. Hopefully, his moving was coming to an end.

That knot in my stomach was getting worse as I listened to Deeanna.

In my mind, I had moved on to "This was only a test of the emergency God-obedience system. We're done with the foster-care system. We're back in control of our lives and our own family."

John was thrilled. I wasn't.

Deeanna and I made plans to go meet Joshua the next day. John had important work meetings that day, and the kids were at school. Deeanna, as head of a Christian child-placement agency, was acting in her official capacity in taking me to meet this little guy.

John and the kids were bubbling over with excitement the night before I met Joshua. Though I still felt hesitant, their excitement was contagious, and I began to share in it—just a little bit.

Joshua's current foster mom had two boys by birth and wanted to adopt a little girl. She felt as though she was getting attached to this little guy, so she wanted to get him into an at-risk adoption family as soon as possible.

Deeanna and I drove up to the house together. I still had a sinking feeling in my stomach. I couldn't stop thinking about how life was so good right now, and this child could have an attachment disorder or other gigantic problems.

I don't want to do this, I thought.

Here's the other thing that was weighing heavily on my mind. (Please don't judge me.) I need sleep. Plenty of it. Lots of it, really. I am a monster without enough sleep. I'm the crabbiest person you'll ever meet without adequate sleep. I knew it was selfish of me, but I was quite concerned about even more sleep disruption.

We went into the house. It was small and fairly run down. It was tidy enough, but it felt old and cramped and dark to me.

The foster mom, a blonde woman in her thirties, was nice but rather abrupt.

"There he is," she said, gesturing across the room.

Joshua was sitting in a little kiddie chair, staring at the TV screen with a juice box in his hand. And he was the cutest stinkin' little thing ever.

At that moment, I think I already loved him.

I'm not kidding you. My heart melted instantly. I said hi to him. He looked at me with the biggest brown eyes and eyelashes you've ever seen. He didn't really talk, but I think he smiled.

I looked at the foster mom, and a smile crept up on my face.

"He's a great sleeper," she said. "He sleeps about twelve hours a night and takes naps."

It was as if she were an angel from God, assuring me that this was our boy, and God was, indeed, right there with me all the way. I just needed to trust Him. I interacted with Joshua as best I could and just spent time sitting on the ground with him. We sat and looked at each other. Then Deeanna and I left, scheming and planning how this little guy could get a forever home.

I was practically skipping. I started the day with two kids, and now I loved three. How was that possible? How did God do that? How could I feel that? It was incredible.

15

"A Stranger Among Us"

John and the kids couldn't wait to meet Joshua. We prayed for him as a family and made plans to visit and take him fishing. According to his foster mom, Joshua had been excited about a picture book they'd been going through that included fishing. So fishing it was. It sounded like a great plan at the time.

We picked up Joshua, and John and the kids were so thrilled. John thought Joshua was adorable. Daniel and Anna were so kind, gentle, and helpful as they interacted with him. Soon we were at the ocean's edge trying to fish. Trying, because, well, we're not fishing people. We really had no idea how to fish, and what seemed like a good idea quickly turned into a not-so-fun experience. Every two seconds all the kids' hooks were getting caught on rocks, corral, and each other, and John had to spend pretty much the entire time fixing everything.

No one was catching any fish. The kids were getting frustrated. John was getting frustrated. It certainly wasn't the fairy-tale outing with our new son that we'd hoped for. We ended up taking Joshua back to his house. We weren't really "feeling" according to the plan.

But that's one of the lessons God was teaching us. We live not by our feelings but by faith. Even though the feelings weren't there, God's direction and peace to proceed were strong and steady.

We chalked up the not-very-good first outing to the stress of the new situation and didn't think too much about it.

As part of the transition plan, we all began to spend more and more time incorporating Joshua into our family. We went to parks and the beach, and we brought him to our house so that he would get familiar with the surroundings and spend time with us at what would soon be his new home.

And an interesting dynamic began to emerge.

The time and attention we were spending getting to know Joshua was time and attention we weren't spending on Daniel and Anna. In all honesty, we started to feel a little resentful toward Joshua over it, even though we knew in our minds how ridiculous those feelings were. Things during the transition period didn't always "feel" right or good, but this time was important for Joshua's well-being, to minimize the shock of moving from one life and home to the next. It's hard to even imagine how hard that experience is for children in foster care.

One of those transition times with Joshua sticks out in my mind. We brought him to our home. Daniel and Anna played beautifully with him. Even though Joshua barely spoke, which made communication and parenting quite difficult for us, Daniel and Anna seemed to know what he meant, and they acted as little translators for us.

I'll never forget having him at our home that weekend for his first sleepover and realizing that he had pooped in his diaper. Remember, he was almost four years old and pretty big at this point. I am admittedly the most squeamish person I know. Obviously, dealing with poopy diapers like this was a challenging experience for me.

But I remember very clearly the Lord speaking to my heart as I took Joshua inside to clean him up.

Here I am to worship . . .

You know the tune. *Here I am to bow down; here I am to say that you're my God.*[1] The song filled my thoughts.

I loved singing that praise song at our church. In that moment, however, I felt the Lord remind me that even the act of changing the diaper of a little boy could be an act of worship. I needed that reminder because when it came to changing dirty diapers, I'd rather have been doing almost anything else.

The transition went quickly. It was only about two weeks from the time John and I received Deeanna's call to the moment we brought Joshua home forever. It was Friday, June 2, 2006. John and I took off from work and went to pick up Joshua while Daniel and Anna stayed home with a sitter.

We couldn't wait to get Joshua out of his foster home. His foster mom cried. We were grateful that she had cared for him. We pulled away from that neighborhood as fast as was appropriate, praising God that we could finally get on with the next phase of our lives.

Because we rented our house on the church and school grounds and John was the administrator, we were blessed to be able to use the grounds as our own little family playground. When we pulled into our driveway, Daniel and Anna came out of the house and asked if they could all go to the playground together.

"Absolutely!" we said.

So there John and I were, standing on the side of the playground watching our new son, who'd been through terrible trauma, laughing and running back and forth across the playground with his new brother and sister.

---

1. Tim Hughes, "Here I Am to Worship," copyright © 2001 by EMI Gospel.

It had been about an eight-month journey from when we first saw those African faces at church to this moment. For Joshua, no more moves. No more trauma. No more uncertain future. He was home. He had the hugest smile on his face that we had ever seen.

And John and I were feeling . . . despondent.

Yes, you read that right. We were both completely and utterly despondent. Despair seeped into our hearts and minds, and we had no idea why. And then, of course, we had guilt over our feelings of despondency. Because, after all, why should we feel that way? An orphan boy was finally home. We had obeyed the call of God on our lives. We had another son.

Why were we feeling this way?

Thankfully, Daniel and Anna seemed relatively unaffected by our feelings. They were enthusiastic the whole way through, and God really used their joy to minister to John and me.

Looking back on that dark time, one of the blessings, again, was the unity John and I had even in the pain. Had one or the other of us felt more "normal" while the other went through these strange feelings, I fear it could have caused a rift in our marriage.

As it was, we leaned on each other. I cried; we prayed and tried to trust God that we were going through this trial so that one day we could be a blessing to others. Even now, that is our prayer in sharing this difficult chapter of our lives. We loved Joshua so much and didn't want to feel this way, but we did.

One day, John described how he felt to me in this way: "It feels like there's a stranger among us."

We had been a tight-knit little family of four, desperately close, loving each other, spending so much of our time just with each other. And now there was someone else. It just felt different. It didn't feel right.

One Saturday I was preparing to speak in a church to encourage

Christians to welcome home legal orphan children trapped in foster care. I was crying out to God, asking Him how I could do that in good conscience when I was a miserable wretch, feeling so downcast from our most recent adoption.

I was reviewing the familiar Scripture verses for the talk. Psalm 68:5–6 says that God is a "father to the fatherless" and that He "sets the lonely in families." James 1:27 says that pure religion is about caring for orphans and widows. Jesus said in Matthew 18:5 that if you welcome a child in His name, you welcome Him. Proverbs 23:10 and Psalm 10:18 tell us to defend and advocate for orphans.

And then came a fresh word of encouragement from Matthew 25:31–45. In verse 35, Jesus said, "For I was hungry and you gave me something to eat, I was thirsty and you gave me something to drink, I was a stranger and you invited me in." Verse 40 says, "Whatever you did for one of the least of these brothers of mine, you did for me." When I read those verses, I felt as if a two-by-four had hit me in the face.

There was a stranger among us, and we took him in. It was good. It was right. It was as if we'd taken in Jesus Himself. John and I were greatly encouraged by that passage of Scripture.

Another moment of encouragement came when I was talking to an adoptive dad, friend, and colleague who'd adopted five children. One of his children had come home within the past two years, and he told me it took eighteen months before he and his wife felt like their family was normal again. Perhaps John and I weren't alone in having these strange and unwanted feelings. We sure felt alone, though.

The unfortunate truth is that pain and difficulty associated with adoption are rarely discussed. There is shame involved, and that shame leads to isolation and silence—the opposite of God's plan for our lives and for His church.

I confided in Deeanna about my feelings, of course, but she just couldn't relate. Deeanna and her husband had had dozens of kids in and out of their home over the years, but she had never struggled with these kinds of feelings. Her family norm was constant change; kids in and out through the decades.

By this time, John and I had adopted three times, and we knew dozens of other families who had adopted. But no one we knew ever talked about going through this kind of disconnect with their child. Other struggles, yes, but not this particular struggle. To be honest, I think John and I felt a pressure to act as though everything was fine, since we were Christians. Somehow we felt these struggles indicated that we were being unfaithful. Looking back, we know that this kind of thinking wasn't true, but it felt true for us at the time.

I wish I could write that we passed through this difficult time quickly. Unfortunately, it took a very long time before our feelings changed. But God used that exceedingly painful and unwanted time in our lives to continue teaching us that we live by faith, not our feelings. He also taught us humility and dependence on Him.

We settled on the fact that we would simply need to trust God and the truth of His Word. We still don't know why we experienced those feelings of despondency. The Bible says that we go through trials and receive the comfort of God so that we can comfort others in their grief (2 Corinthians 1:3–4). That's all we could figure. It seems like a pat and tidy answer. But in truth, it's neither pat nor tidy. It was messy, and it was hard. And we developed a tad more spiritual toughness, if you will.

We came to the conclusion that either we believed what we said or we didn't. We had to choose God and trust Him—one day, sometimes one moment, at a time. By God's grace, we didn't give up. And eventually it got much, much better. I was always thankful that God had given me a glimpse of that normal, loving motherly feeling on the first day I met Joshua. At the time, I had no idea it would be awhile before I felt it again, but those normal, loving parent feelings did eventually return for both John and me.

Having gone through that difficult experience, John and I feel strongly that folks going through the same thing need to reach out and talk to others, seek professional help, or join a support group. This kind of struggle is more common than you think, and you aren't alone. Cling to hope because there *is* hope. Lots of it, actually. We had a hard time believing that when we were struggling to feel bonded with Joshua, but it's absolutely true.

Don't give up, and don't live by your feelings. If some of your family and friends are offering only judgment and unsolicited—and unhelpful—advice, give yourself permission to enforce healthy boundaries with them.

Instead, seek comfort from trustworthy, godly friends, and find a good counselor who specializes in adoption-related issues. Asking for help is key to finding strength. (You'll find more information about finding a counselor in the resources section at the back of the book.)

We know from Scripture that God's grace is sufficient for us and that *His* power is made perfect in our weakness (2 Corinthians 12:9). He can and will work through your weakness in this type of trial.

John and I were kept afloat, in part, by dear friends, including Deeanna and one of our best friends ever, Chris.

Chris was in our small group and was an assistant pastor at our church. In Hawaii, all adults in a child's life are referred to as "uncle" or "auntie." Chris was known in our home as "Uncle Pastor Chris." He had an incredible life and testimony. Before he became a Christian, he was addicted to drugs and spent time in a psychiatric institution. He eventually became a pastor. He married, but his wife left him. He raised his two children as a single dad and led countless people to Christ. He would later remarry a lovely, godly woman who would become our close friend as well.

Years later, he baptized Daniel and Anna in the Pacific Ocean; it was his last pastoral act before he went home unexpectedly to be with his Lord. He was only fifty-one. We miss him desperately and will always be grateful to him for his friendship and support when we needed it most.

Looking back over this difficult time in our lives, I know that just like all parents, we failed at times and succeeded at times. We made mistakes more often than we'd care to admit. It pains John and me to think about this time. Joshua deserved better parents than us, with our struggling feelings. But to this day, we hold to God's truth about this time and how much we learned from it. We're thankful for God's forgiveness of our failures, and we trust that God will use this trial to encourage others.

As I mentioned earlier, this was considered an at-risk adoption situation, which meant that the rights of Joshua's birth parents hadn't yet been legally terminated. So Joshua still had visits with his birth mother, and I took him to them.

I would have thought there was no way I could do such a thing.

Before our first visit, I felt nervous and intimidated, like I had to compete with his other mom, his "real" mom. (Of course, "real" parents are those who . . . well, parent. We were and are Joshua's real parents. But I couldn't help feeling intimidated by the situation.) I wasn't sure what to expect during that initial visit, but my fears and jealousies, if you will, quickly disappeared when I met Joshua's birth mother.

We were to meet at a playground, and Joshua and I were already there playing. A city bus pulled up, and his birth mother got off.

A Department of Human Services worker was also there to supervise the visit and make sure things went well. Joshua's birth mother walked very, very slowly toward us.

Interestingly, Joshua expressed no change in emotion. He was happy enough playing on the equipment and never reacted any differently toward her than he did when anyone else approached. I never did and still don't know for sure what to make of that. Maybe he had grieved the loss during his year in foster care and had moved on. Or maybe he just didn't recognize her. He didn't seem to remember anything about her.

I expected her to be rather antagonistic toward me, with an attitude like "Who is this woman trying to take my son?"

But she wasn't.

She moved as if she were in slow motion. She had long brown hair and beautiful brown skin, a classic Micronesian, Pacific-Islander look. She was nice, shy, and very gentle, but again, moving almost in slow motion. I think it was the combination of the effects of drugs, alcohol, and just her personality.

I would sit to the side, and she would slowly follow Joshua around the playground, smiling rarely and not really connecting with him. He seemed oblivious, just playing the whole time and not really connecting with her either. It was the oddest thing.

We continued these visits once a week. Even though she faithfully came to the visits for the most part, she wasn't doing any of the other things DHS required of her in order to get her son back.

It was clear where this was headed: Her rights would be terminated. Joshua's birth father was out of the picture, addicted to drugs and living on the streets back on the mainland.

My heart softened toward Joshua's birth mother. I felt badly for her. After one of the visits, I offered to drive her back to Waikiki so she didn't have to ride the bus again. She shyly accepted and sat next to Joshua in the backseat.

He fell asleep (that's my boy!), and she kept saying in her broken English, "He so happy; he so happy." I think she noticed how peaceful he looked, and it pleased her. In her way, she clearly loved him. But she wasn't willing or wasn't able to make the changes necessary to be the mother he needed.

Through our conversation that day, I learned that she wasn't with Joshua's father any longer but had a new boyfriend. I also learned, alarmingly, that this new boyfriend was violent with her. I encouraged her to leave him and let me drive her to a domestic-violence shelter. She declined, seeming hopeless and trapped.

I wanted to protect her, to make her get help, but I couldn't. She got out and thanked me for taking care of Joshua. She had been so pleased he was going to church and was in a Christian school. I asked her to reconsider and get away from the violent boyfriend. She just looked at me with blank eyes and closed the door, mumbling another "Thank you."

She showed up at the next week's visit with a present for Joshua— a Hawaiian shirt and little matching shorts. She seemed to try to hug him more than usual, and she was teary. When the hour was up and she said good-bye, it felt different than usual.

I had my suspicions. I'd seen and heard about this kind of thing before. I thought it would be her last good-bye. She'd made clear by her actions that she wasn't going to try to get him back. But this seemed to be the end. Perhaps I was wrong, but I had an instinct.

And sure enough, that's what it was.

She never came to another visit after that or responded to DHS in any way. Her parental rights were terminated, as well as the birth father's. The way seemed clear for us to adopt Joshua.

16

"All We Want for Christmas Is . . ."

I t was fall 2006, and we were really hoping Joshua's adoption would be finalized before Christmas. What a gift that would be! It's hard to describe how desperately we longed for adoption finalization to become a reality. It may seem like just a formality, but the unconscious stress involved can really take its toll. Consider the reality: Life is totally unsettled, others seem—and are—in control of the biggest thing in your life, and it is an incredible faith walk.

Before finalization, everything you know about your life and child can change in an instant for any or no reason. DHS could show up at any time and change your future. Your children, who love each other, could lose their sibling. It wasn't likely for us at this point, but we knew it was still possible.

After adoption finalization, that fear is finally over. You wait no more for your future to finally begin. You can exhale. You can breathe. It's beautiful relief.

As we prayed for this moment to come with Joshua, we had two fascinating encounters with his birth relatives. One was a peek into his past; the other a preview to the future.

Deeanna had told us that Joshua's birth mother had a cousin named Sara from Micronesia who was a wonderful Christian woman. Sara and her husband lived on Oahu and ministered together at a local rescue mission.

I asked Deeanna why Sara wasn't going to adopt Joshua. She told me it was because Sara had several children already, and her husband had been critically ill recently. He was finally recovering, but they just didn't have the ability to parent another child.

Our church had a great relationship with the same rescue mission that Sara was involved with. People from the mission would come to our church about once a year and update the congregation on all the wonderful work they were doing ministering to homeless families and children. When I found out they were coming again to our church, I swung into action to see if Sara would be on the visiting team this year.

I was so excited to find out she was!

In addition to Sunday services, our church had a Friday night service, too. So right after dinner that particular Friday, we headed to church about an hour early, knowing that the rescue-mission team would be setting up and preparing for the service. We were nervous and excited. We wanted Sara to see how well Joshua was doing. Deeanna knew Sara and had told her all about us. Deeanna said Sara was excited to meet us and see Joshua again.

When we got to church, we quickly learned that Sara wasn't there yet, so we went into the sanctuary to wait for her with our family of five. John and I sat in the pew while the kids played around us, joking and laughing. Not too long after we sat down, we noticed two women from the mission (neither of whom was Sara) staring at Joshua.

We smiled, and they began to walk toward us somewhat shyly. Then we noticed they were both crying. They approached Joshua and began to talk to him.

They seemed to know him.

We quickly stood up and introduced ourselves, smiling to put them at ease but growing even more curious. What was this about?

We explained that we were Joshua's parents and that we expected to be adopting him soon. We introduced Daniel and Anna and told the ladies that this was our home church and that we were waiting to meet Sara.

The tears were really flowing now, and it took awhile for these ladies to tell their story.

"God is so faithful; we just can't even believe it," said the more talkative of the two, a gentle and kind woman in her sixties.

"We prayed so hard for him," she continued.

"We bought him his stroller," the shy one, a local woman in her forties, chimed in.

"We know his birth parents. They were homeless when he was a baby. They came to the mission regularly. We gave them food. We were so worried about him," the older woman said as they stared at Joshua.

"We didn't know what to do about Joshua . . . if we should call the authorities or not. We prayed so hard for him," she repeated. "He was always crawling in the grass. That's why we bought him the stroller. We prayed that God would do a miracle for him and protect him, and we prayed for his future." The woman sniffled.

John and I were flabbergasted.

"We're rejoicing that God has allowed us to see the answer to our prayers," she said.

Just then, we heard a loud shriek. We turned to see a beautiful woman with long brown hair and beautiful brown skin moving quickly toward Joshua.

Before we knew it, she had him in her arms and was kissing his head, saying, "I can't believe it, I can't believe it." It was Sara.

We introduced ourselves and spent some time talking with her. She was as kind as she could be and so grateful that the Lord set this lonely boy in our family. She was adamant that he was where he belonged. It was so encouraging to us.

We all prayed together, marveling at God's answers to all our prayers. We don't always know or get to see those answers, but that night we did—all of us did.

We never saw Sara again, but we appreciated the peek into Joshua's past. With our three kids and two jobs, and Sara's many children, a sick husband, and her active ministry to Honolulu's homeless families, we just never had the time to stay in touch. But I suspect she, like us, felt our encounter that day was a gift from God.

A glimpse into our future with one of Joshua's birth relatives began with, what else, a phone call from Joshua's social worker. About five months before we met Sara, we received a phone call about Joshua's birth grandmother.

It turned out the mother of Joshua's birth father (Joshua's grandmother) had learned that he was in foster care and had been frantically calling child-welfare officials to find him and confirm that he was okay. Kathy lived in Ohio, and I was told to expect a call from her. She had never met Joshua before, and when she had been contacted about raising him, she didn't feel she was in a position to parent a small child, even if he was her grandchild.

The social worker thought Kathy would be okay with us adopting Joshua, but told us that Kathy wanted to talk to us first to make sure she felt good about his new home.

John and I weren't so sure how we felt about all of this. We weren't too keen on having our kids' past connections colliding with our family's future. If the decision had been based only on our preference, we'd have politely said, "No, thank you," and declined this opportunity to connect with Kathy. But had we said that, she likely would have objected to the adoption and thrown our future into uncertainty. So, as with all these new milestones in our lives, the Lord seemed to have His hand at our back, and we were carried along regardless of our feelings.

Grandma Kathy was kind, but she was also fierce in protecting Joshua's future. She made it quite clear that she wanted to stay involved in his life, or she wouldn't consent to the adoption.

We were fine with that, but we had a requirement too—a requirement that might have tripped up a lesser woman.

"You can be a grandma to Joshua his whole life, but here's the thing: You have to be a grandma to all our kids, not just him. They are a unit. We're a team, and we don't want anything causing division among the kids," I explained.

I waited less than a second for a response.

"Absolutely!" Kathy said. "Now I have three grandkids," she declared without missing a beat.

She was resolute. She would love them all equally. Because we were all the way across the ocean, we could only speak by phone and wouldn't meet in person for a few years. But I can tell you that she has kept her word. She truly loves all our kids, and if you were to watch her interact with them to this day, you'd never know which one is her birth grandchild. She loves them all. And they love her.

After that glimpse into our future with Grandma Kathy, God granted our prayer, and on December 12, 2006, we finalized the adoption of Joshua John Rosati. The judge was an adoptive dad himself, and it was a really special ceremony. He gave a Joshua a stuffed toy dog that to this day is his "adoption dog."

My dad and his family were there with us, and we went out for a special lunch after court, which had become a family tradition. This time we went to a hotel in Waikiki and ate right by the ocean. The Christmas decorations made it extra special, and we thanked God for the best Christmas present ever—our son Joshua.

17

Fighting for
a Cause

I need to flash back now to the year 2001 and tell you about my work at the Hawaii Family Forum. You may be tempted to zone out, but stay with me. It's a highly relevant and dramatic reminder of the ways God weaved together the seemingly unconnected events in our lives.

One of my tasks as the executive director of HFF was to advance pro-family bills in the Hawaii legislature. Early in my tenure, I received a note from an elderly gentleman asking for my help to raise Hawaii's age of sexual consent. His note explained that Hawaii had the lowest age of sexual consent in the nation—a minor could consent at just fourteen years of age. As a practical matter, this meant that a man of any age could legally have sex with a fourteen-year-old girl. In no other state was this legal. For most states, the age of sexual consent was at least sixteen.

The main purpose of age-of-consent laws is to protect minors from adult sexual exploitation. The idea is that a child doesn't have the maturity or capacity to legally "consent" to have sex with adults. These laws are also known as statutory rape laws.

I was shocked when I read the constituent's letter, and my first reaction was that he must be wrong. I did some research, however, and discovered that he was right.

This is outrageous. People must not know, I reasoned. *Regardless of one's political perspective, surely everyone will agree on this. I'll just educate legislators. I'll fix this.*

I set up a meeting with the chairwoman of the key senate committee that had jurisdiction over these types of issues and explained the situation to her. She seemed alarmed that this could be true. She said she'd look into it. In the meantime, she wanted me to meet with the leaders of Hawaii's women's movement.

I was happy to do that. Granted, as a sanctity-of-human-life and pro-family advocate, I did battle with the same women on other legislative issues, such as abortion. I didn't really know many of these women personally; we had just testified against one another in senate hearings. But I was happy to be able to find a topic we could work together on—especially for the sake of protecting Hawaii's young women. *This is a great opportunity,* I thought.

The senator called the meeting, and I was up close and personal with women who believed that I was the voice of regression who wanted to strip them of their reproductive health-care rights.

They smiled very nicely and then proceeded to explain why keeping the age of sexual consent at fourteen was actually "a good thing."

I was flabbergasted. They explained that you couldn't really stop sex between adult men and teenage girls.

"And, well, there's a cultural component," they said.

"And, well, police have better things to do with limited law-enforcement resources," they continued.

"And, well, if a fourteen-year-old can get access to birth control and abortion without her parents' knowledge, then she also needs the autonomy to have sex with whomever she wants, however old he is."

Bingo. There was the real reason. It was all about abortion rights in their minds.

I completely disagreed with what they said, but I could at least comprehend their sad logic.

In turn, I wondered, could they at least understand my perspective, even if they couldn't agree with it? Could they see that young girls might be exploited by older men? And weren't they concerned with the "grooming" that went on when older men seduced young women by being their "boyfriends," only to lure them into the commercial sex industry?

Unfortunately, no. They said they couldn't even understand where I was coming from. I felt as if I were living on Mars. I couldn't understand why these women wouldn't see reason. But with an established women's group so opposed to raising the age of consent, I was dead in the water. They were very powerful in Hawaii.

If that weren't bad enough, the last people in the world you'd ever expect were also opposed to our efforts to raise the age of sexual consent—some of the law-enforcement community.

I was dumbfounded.

The very people with a protective mind set—the police and prosecutors—put on a full-court press to oppose raising the age. I couldn't believe it. *Are you serious?* I fumed. Their public rationale was that it's too hard to prosecute, girls won't cooperate, and so on. But there was another reason: They worked closely with the women's groups who also opposed changing the law.

To me, this was madness. Something had to give.

Around that same time, the political party out of power had a promising prospect for governor and more seats than they'd had in a long time in the House of Representatives. They had also started talking about the age-of-consent issue.

So, we at the Hawaii Family Forum decided to go over the heads of the legislature and appeal directly to the people of Hawaii. Surely they didn't know about this, and if they did, they'd want to protect their girls.

Thankfully, we were right. The main Honolulu paper ran an editorial I had written on the topic, and the issue began to pick up steam in the media. With all the media attention, legislators suddenly didn't want to appear to be on the same side as sexual predators—especially with an upcoming election. After significant effort, which had begun more than a year before, and thanks to many helpful legislators and community members, the legislature passed a bill to raise Hawaii's age of sexual consent from fourteen to sixteen.

What a victory! All we needed now was for the governor to sign it or allow it to become law without his signature, and the girls of Hawaii would have greater protection. In a shocking move, however, the governor vetoed the bill. That's right; he *vetoed* the bill.

The only chance we had now would be for the legislature to override the veto of a governor from the same party—oh, just something that hadn't happened since before *statehood* (1959)!

If ever there was a truly impossible task, this was it.

But if I've learned anything, it's the truth that nothing is impossible with God. He allowed me the incredible privilege of brokering the deal between key members of the majority and minority leadership teams in the House of Representatives to call the legislature back into session and override the veto.

And they did it. They really did it!

It was a huge media story, and those of us involved were so

thankful to the Lord for His incredible mercy and grace. Later, the *Honolulu Star-Bulletin* blessed me by naming me as one of the ten people who made a difference in the state that year for the age-of-consent effort.

Now, why did I tell you this story?

Fast-forward to 2006. The cause that had been my life for some time (raising the age of sexual consent) was now the law of the land in Hawaii. Laws and social policy affect lives and families. That's why people advance their ideas and worldviews. I know this; it's why I was a lobbyist for pro-family causes. But I was about to experience this truth in a way I never could have expected.

18

Missing and
Exploited

I t had been more than five years since the age-of-consent law was
passed, and John and I were about to see firsthand how well the
change in law was being implemented. It was July 2006, and
we were living in Manoa, Honolulu, Hawaii, near the University of
Hawaii and not too far from our church, John's workplace, and the
legislature.

We had to move from our Kaimuki house once we adopted
Joshua because it simply wasn't big enough for a family of five. John
was still working full-time as the Kaimuki Christian Church and
School administrator. At this time, I was running the Hawaii Family
Forum part-time from home. We had a wonderful Christian woman
helping us with chores and shopping. Life was full, and we were still
adjusting to having three children.

One day a friend of ours, Doris, called me crying. Their daughter Emma, whom they had adopted from foster care at age twelve,
was really struggling. I knew and loved Emma. I can't disclose too
many details, but suffice it to say that her story of childhood abuse

and neglect was one of the most harrowing I had ever heard—and I'd heard a lot in my line of work.

Doris and her husband had fought to keep Emma safe, had adopted her, and had tried to give her a wonderful life. Emma had accepted Christ and was even active in youth group. But now she was fourteen and was really struggling with all that had happened in her past.

Emma wouldn't go to counseling any longer, and she stopped going to church. She was shutting down and had begun running away. Doris had been really worried, praying fervently for Emma and loving her with the fierceness of a determined mother.

She enrolled Emma in a local martial-arts class, hoping the experience would help build her self-worth and provide her with an activity she was interested in. And it really did seem to be good for Emma. The instructor, Bill, was a forty-year-old man, and his interest in her and her interest in the classes seemed to be helping. Emma was perking up a bit.

One day when Doris went to pick her up, she found Emma and Bill off to the side, laughing and joking. Doris immediately got that "mom sense" in the pit of her stomach and knew something wasn't right. It just wasn't appropriate for a man Bill's age to be interacting with their fourteen-year-old in this way. Doris talked to Emma, to Bill, and to the management. She made her concerns clear, and everyone assured her that there was nothing going on.

But Emma began sneaking out of the house more and more, and one day Doris intercepted a series of text messages between Emma and Bill. Her worst fears were confirmed. This forty-year-old man was sexually exploiting their fourteen-year-old daughter.

Not long before this, Bill's relationship with Emma would have been legal in Hawaii, but since the higher age of sexual consent had been passed by the legislature, this man was committing a serious crime. And Doris had the text messages as proof that there was inappropriate behavior going on.

She went to the police, but they were completely nonchalant about the whole thing and wouldn't help. She badgered them, and finally the officers said they'd come talk to her daughter. Talk to her daughter? Why didn't they go talk to Bill, the forty-year-old man who was exploiting her? She couldn't believe it. One police officer told Doris and her husband, Russell, that this situation was akin to being unable to make Emma eat her oatmeal.

Did he just compare this situation to Emma eating her oatmeal? Doris thought. *This is crazy. They're blaming the victim!*

The whole thing seemed surreal.

Doris was desperate. She knew something bad was going to happen, but she couldn't do anything to stop it. She and her husband took drastic action, like putting an alarm on Emma's bedroom door and watching her like a hawk during their waking hours to prevent her from running away. Every time Emma had run away before, Doris and Russell had always been able to find her and bring her home. But one night Emma managed to slip out with Bill, and they couldn't find her.

Doris and Russell printed flyers, called the police, and canvassed the airport. It did no good. Emma was gone. Bill had taken her. A forty-year-old man had their fourteen-year-old daughter, and there was nothing they could do about it.

Emma was eventually put on the national registry for missing and exploited children. Her parents didn't know whether she was dead or alive for more than two years.

19

You Can Never Have Enough Hope

I stopped asking Doris if they'd heard anything about Emma because I didn't want to bring up a painful topic. I just waited and prayed and figured she'd tell me if they had news. And eventually she did.

"Kelly, we found Emma," she called me one day, full of excitement.

"What?" I said.

"We got a call last night from Bill," she said.

"Are you kidding? Where are they?" I replied.

"They've been in Puerto Rico, and Kelly, they have a baby," Doris said.

"A baby? Oh my gosh!" I gasped.

"Yes, a little girl. Her name is Hope. But Emma took off and left Bill two nights ago. She went to do drugs with another guy and left the baby with Bill. He didn't know what to do. He can't take care of her," she explained.

"I can't believe he had the nerve to call you," I said.

"He's at his wit's end and says he's coming back here so we can help with the baby. When Emma found out he's coming back to Hawaii, she said she'll come, too. So they're all coming back tomorrow," she said.

Shortly after Emma, Bill, and baby Hope returned to Hawaii, Emma, now a confused seventeen-year-old, ran away again to do drugs and live on the beach. Bill now wanted Doris and her husband to take care of Hope because he couldn't. He said he was too tired at the end of his workdays to care for Hope. She had so much energy and was just too hard for him to handle alone.

What a messy situation.

Doris and her husband decided to take their two-year-old granddaughter into their home, even though they already had several children who were adopted or in foster care, and they were active in ministry.

But taking care of Hope quickly turned into a terrible experience. She was completely out of control from a lack of parenting, and she was consuming their lives—destabilizing their home, their marriage, and the other children.

I was on the phone one day with Doris after they'd had Hope for about six months, and I was trying to offer her support and encouragement. Doris was whimpering a little but not full-on crying.

"We've come to the hard reality that we're going to have to find an adoptive family for Hope," she said to me, sniffling.

"Oh, honey, I'm so sorry! That must be really hard," I responded as empathetically as I could.

"And there's only one family"—sniffle, sniffle—"in the whole wide world"—sniffle, sniffle—"that we'd ever trust our granddaughter with," sniffle, sniffle.

I literally felt my stomach twirl. *Oh no.* I knew where this was going.

"Who do you mean, honey? Yourself, right? You can only trust her with yourself," I offered hopefully.

"No." Now she was really crying. *"You!"* she said.

I couldn't speak. *Oh, Lord, have mercy. What in the world am I going to tell her?*

Silence on my end.

Crying on hers.

Finally, I mustered the courage to speak. "Oh, Doris, we're still right in the middle of this crazy bonding struggle with Joshua," I told her. "I don't see any possible way we could adopt Hope."

She didn't say anything.

"Uh . . . I'll talk to John, but I sure don't think we could ever do that. I'm so sorry, sweetie. But I will talk to John," I blurted out.

I don't remember how we ended our conversation. I just remember hanging up the phone and nearly laughing to myself at the absurdity of her suggestion. Of course, I would tell John. I was sure he would think I'd lost my mind for even bringing it up.

I marched out to the carport to find John. He had also been praying for our friends and wanted to know the latest information.

"You won't believe what Doris just said to me," I told him. I proceeded to recount the conversation, ending with the bombshell that Doris and Russell wanted us to adopt Hope.

"Can you believe that?" I asked him incredulously.

I was fully expecting John to say, "Are they crazy?"

Instead, my husband looked straight at me, shrugged his shoulders, and uttered the words I'll never forget: "Whatever the Lord has for us."

I was stunned by his openness in the midst of our ongoing struggle with Joshua, but as we chatted away into the evening about the possibility, it was as if the Lord was reminding us that in our own pain, we needed to remember to reach out, not pull in.

You might be reading this thinking that we're adrenaline junkies who have some psychological attachment to drama and to being needed. All I can say is that John and I wanted more than anything to follow God's will for us and our family. We had a holy fear of acting outside God's will, so we agreed to pray that He would show us what that was.

20

Is Our Table
Big Enough?

A s we prayed and talked about possibly adopting Hope, one of our biggest concerns was that we didn't view "openness" in adoption quite the same way Doris and Russell did. When it comes to adoption, people have different views and preferences. John and I were comfortable with a degree of openness, to be sure, but not the degree that Doris and Russell advocated.

For example, Doris and Russell wanted all of us to attend family functions together and have Hope call both Emma and me "Mom." I just wasn't comfortable with that. Of course, Hope would know her story, have Doris and Russell in her life, and know that Emma loved her very much. But we weren't comfortable agreeing up front to Hope having regular contact with Emma.

We feared that our different perspectives could set us up for failure and frustration, even resentment and anger, so we talked to Doris and Russell directly about it. John and I were completely in sync about this. We explained that we believed in open communication, but the only thing we could commit to was keeping everyone informed and always acting in Hope's best interest, as we determined it by God's grace.

Let me clarify that we don't suggest that our approach is best for everyone, but we felt strongly that it was best for our family.

Doris and Russell gently tried to help us see their perspective, but they didn't change our minds. They were okay with that and even joked that none of their children ever take their advice. We love Doris and Russell, and our strong friendship formed the foundation of trust that allowed us all to go forward, even though we didn't have the exact same perspective.

With that crucial conversation behind us, we were willing to meet little Hope and help in whatever way God showed us, from providing respite care to being her forever family or anything in between. As we drove the forty-five minutes across the island that Saturday afternoon to meet Hope, we only told the kids that we were going to visit Doris and her family and meet their little grand-daughter, who was staying with them.

Emma was still on the run and using drugs during this time. Doris cared for Hope throughout the week, and Bill picked her up and took care of her for part of the weekend. Bill was scheduled to bring Hope back that weekend shortly after we arrived at Doris's house. When Bill pulled up in his broken-down truck, we were sitting on the couch with Doris in an outside room. (In Hawaii, it's common to have furnished rooms outside because of the warm weather.) You can imagine the different emotions we had toward Bill—we were angry for everything he'd put Doris's family through and for taking Emma to begin with. Meeting him was a strange moment for us.

"John and Kelly, this is Bill," Doris introduced us.

"Uh, nice to meet you," he mumbled in a barely audible voice,

his head careening wildly as he tried to keep track of his rambunc-
tious daughter. We stood and shook his hand. "Nice to meet you,
too," we struggled to say.

And then we saw her.

It was a moment we'll never forget. She was dressed only in a
dirty diaper, which was hanging halfway off her tiny body. Not another stitch of clothing. No shoes. She was dirty. Her hair was wild
and sticking out from all sides of her head. She was climbing on top
of the furniture like a monkey. Without warning, John and I both
smiled and were taken instantly with this little creature. Wow, was
she cute. And naughty.

"Hope, get down! Hope, stop doing that!" Bill was barking.

Hope wasn't listening. Bill was way out of his league with this
child.

But despite her unruly behavior, with her brown skin, exotic
brown eyes, and curly hair, she was as adorable as a child could be.
Our kids found her fascinating and were patient and calm, following
her around and trying to direct her. She was equally fascinated with
them but maintained her wild activity. She tried to bite all of them
and frequently screamed and kicked.

Oh boy, I thought, *what have we gotten ourselves into?*

We spent a few hours there that day so we wouldn't be strangers
when we started to care for Hope.

On the car ride home that night, we had the most profound
conversation with Daniel and Anna. After talking about how cute
Hope was and what a rascal she was, Daniel asked, "Where's her
mom?"

"Well, she's making sad choices at the moment, and she's with
her friends instead of taking care of her child," I said.

"That's sad. What about her dad?" Daniel asked.

"Well, he's making some sad choices too, and we don't know if he will be able to take care of Hope," I told him. "We're praying that her mom will make a good choice and take care of Hope, but we don't know if . . ."

Just then, Anna interrupted the conversation. "Mom, so if those grown-ups don't make good choices and take good care of the children, then they shouldn't have the privilege of raising the children," she exclaimed with moral certainty. At this point, Anna was five years old.

"That's exactly right. Her grandparents love her, but they have a house full of kids already, and they might not be able to raise Hope either," I said.

"Mom," Daniel asked, "if she needs to have parents who will take care of her, can we take care of her? She can come live in our family."

"Yeah, she can come with us," Anna said.

Even Joshua piped up from the back, "Yeah!"

John and I were amazed, content, and happy during the dark drive home across Oahu that night, reflecting on how our kids "got it." If Hope needed us, we'd be there for her. That pretty much summed it up. We had no doubt the drama would continue before the situation was resolved, but there was a sweet peace in the car that night.

Just about two months after Joshua's adoption was finalized, we started taking Hope for a few days at a time to give Doris and Russell a break. Those were hard days. At that point in her teensy life, Hope knew and used more foul curse words than most adults I knew. She was just modeling what she'd heard, of course, and had no idea what she was really saying. But we were worried that our other kids would pick up Hope's bad language. Thankfully, that didn't happen.

There were good times, too. The kids loved getting to know Hope, and so did we. She brought a lot of excitement to our house; she clearly loved being the center of attention and having other kids to play with. At Doris and Russell's, the other kids were much older. Hope was often sad when I had to take her back. She was clearly bonding with us—and we were bonding with her.

I rocked her often and fed her from a bottle to help with our bonding. John, especially, was falling hard for this little one. It was always a difficult balance in these situations when we didn't know what the outcome would be. We wanted to give this child our hearts fully and without reservation because that's what she needed. But our self-preservation instincts were also strong, causing us to want to hold back to guard our hearts in case the adoption didn't happen.

This is one of the key places where the rubber meets the road in trusting God and being willing to love like Jesus loves.

We sure didn't always do this well or right, but we wanted to, and we asked God to give us the strength to give all our kids the love they needed. And the respite we provided was a lifeline for Doris and Russell. We were really glad about that.

At this point in the process, child-welfare officials weren't yet involved, and our poor friends were agonizing over what to do. They really wanted their daughter Emma to come back and care for her child. They didn't want to give up on Emma.

They also really wanted to hold Bill accountable for his behavior with Emma. They wanted to contact the police again regarding Bill, because Hope was the proof they needed of his inappropriate relationship with Emma, even if Emma wouldn't cooperate. But they were also concerned about the consequences of taking away Hope's dad now too, since her mom had already left her. It was a really hard situation.

Bill already had an unstable personality, but as he became more desperate about Emma leaving him, he was getting worse. One day Doris learned that Bill had threatened physical violence to Emma's new boyfriend over the phone—with Hope in the car listening to every word. Bill told Doris the whole story, which demonstrated how unstable and unfit he was to be a parent. He didn't even realize how self-incriminating it was to tell Doris all this scary information. He was just desperate to get Emma back.

Our friends realized that if Bill was threatening violence, they couldn't let Hope be alone with him. He had taken Emma and run to Puerto Rico years earlier, and Doris and Russell were concerned that he might take their granddaughter. But without legal intervention, there was no way to keep Hope from her birth father.

Doris and Russell didn't want to provoke Bill into doing something crazy, so they tried to act as though things were all right, holding him off by making excuses about why this time or that wouldn't work for him to spend time with Hope alone.

In the meantime, Hope had been spending more and more of her time with us. The tension was building, and Doris kept making excuses to keep Bill from taking Hope. Doris even tried to talk to him, explaining why it would be best for Hope not to go with him when he was so upset about Emma.

This just made him angry and explosive.

Time was running out. We were all afraid that Bill would try to take Hope and run. On a Friday afternoon, Doris and I worked with an attorney and raced to the courthouse to get a temporary restraining order to buy time to figure this all out.

By God's grace, we got the restraining order just as the courts closed for the weekend. The hearing for the permanent restraining order was set for early the following week. Doris and I were relieved but not convinced that a little piece of paper would stop the man who had absconded with their daughter years earlier.

So to keep Hope safe, we literally hid Doris and Russell that weekend. They left Bill a message that they would be gone for a few days. John and I put our friends up at a Waikiki hotel for the weekend, and we kept Hope with us. Bill didn't know where we lived, and we prayed he wouldn't find out.

He seemed to buy the story, but it was an edgy time. It's a very strange thing to worry about someone showing up and snatching a child. We lived in a quiet cul-de-sac. At one point that weekend, an old truck rolled up in front of our house, and we thought for sure Bill had figured the whole thing out.

Thankfully, it was a false alarm.

Monday couldn't come soon enough.

———— ∞ ————

Even though Doris and her family had been taking care of Hope, their only legal recourse was to try to arrange for guardianship on the basis of their daughter's abandonment and drug use and Bill's general unfitness as evidenced by his conduct with their daughter and his recent inappropriate behavior in front of Hope.

As grandparents, Doris and Russell had a shot at success; we were only outside strangers with no legal standing or opportunity to get custody of Hope. This was such an emotional roller coaster because we just wanted to adopt Hope and move on with our lives and our children.

The outcome we wanted seemed totally outside the realm of possibility from a legal and practical standpoint. It just seemed hopeless. Doris and her husband didn't know how they could raise Hope even if they did win this legal battle for guardianship. Caring for her hadn't worked well when they'd tried it before. They felt sure the Lord had been leading toward placing Hope with us, but with every new circumstance, that outcome seemed more and more impossible.

The day came for the court hearing on their motion for permanent guardianship. Hope was home with us. It was very possible, even likely, that Emma wouldn't show up, since she was still doing drugs and living on the beach. But we figured Bill would show.

Once a judge heard Bill's history with Emma, we hoped that Doris would be able to get permanent guardianship. Then we'd all just have to proceed from there. Hope's safety was paramount, and this was the only way to ensure it at this point.

Waiting for the phone to ring seemed to take forever. Finally it did. Doris was on the line.

"What happened?" I asked.

"Well," she said, "both Emma and Bill showed up, and Emma was furious with us."

"What?" I asked. I couldn't believe my ears. I really didn't think Emma would show up.

Doris continued, "They both fought us, telling the judge lies about us and saying we were unfit to have Hope." My friend was clearly in emotional pain but somehow holding herself together.

"The judge called in child-welfare officials to mediate the dispute and take Hope officially into foster-care custody," Doris responded.

Oh my, I thought to myself. *DHS is now involved. That's both good and bad, and Doris and I know it.*

But Doris also sounded a bit happy, and I couldn't figure out why.

"Kelly, you won't believe what God did."

"What?" I had Hope on my lap, and John was two inches from my face. I was repeating everything she said so he could hear.

"Emma was so furious with me. She said she'd never let us have her daughter. So I asked her, 'What if Auntie Kelly keeps Hope while you get clean?' And, Kelly, she agreed. And because she agreed, Bill agreed, too."

I was speechless.

"And since you've adopted from foster care three times already, you're cleared with DHS. I just need to bring the social worker on the phone to confirm with you that you'll take her as an official foster-care placement," she told me very calmly.

This was truly unbelievable. What seemed humanly impossible had just been made possible by God. He'd done more than we ever could have imagined. It was incredible.

I spoke to the social worker, and our fourth foray into the world of child welfare was officially launched on April 25, 2007.

21

Nothing but
the Facts

Hope was now officially living with us. John and I were still having trouble connecting with Joshua at times, and Hope was the naughtiest little two-year-old we'd ever seen. We had four kids ages six and under.

Life was stressful.

And as John and I dealt with the day-to-day stress of parenting and an uncertain future, another scenario was playing out with Emma and Bill. Emma wanted nothing to do with Bill, and she now had a new boyfriend, another man in his forties whom she'd met on the beach while taking drugs. Bill was still pining for Emma and had never been held accountable for his criminal behavior with Emma. Both of them wanted Hope in their lives, but neither was fit to parent her.

John and I had to take Hope to separate visits with Emma and Bill. Even though we wanted to adopt Hope, we truly were supportive of Emma turning her life around and getting her little girl back. We knew she loved Hope, in her own way, but she just wasn't showing that she could take care of her. She was seventeen at this point and had been afforded the great privilege of being able to enter a drug-court program. This was a separate legal track not available to everyone. It offered intensive in-patient drug rehabilitation, parenting, and life-skills support.

Emma had a court appearance every Friday, and I joined Doris in being there for Emma and cheering her on. We wanted her to be reunited with Hope. A few months into the process, Emma seemed to be making good progress on the drug-rehabilitation front, but her social worker was concerned that she was more focused on her new boyfriend than she was on Hope. Her new boyfriend also wanted to get clean, so he was in rehabilitation as well.

The social worker recommended that the court issue a no-contact order, and the court agreed. This order prohibited Emma from seeing, talking to, or making any contact with her boyfriend (who was also in drug court) so she could focus only on getting clean and becoming a good mother.

Emma agreed to this and seemed compliant. To be honest, Doris and I were doubtful she'd stick with it, but we kept trying to be supportive. Weeks went by, and Emma insisted she'd had no contact with her boyfriend. Doris and I were suspicious, but Emma was adamant, and she was doing well staying off drugs in her in-patient rehab house. We took her to lunch one afternoon after drug court, and she talked on and on about how great she was doing and how well she was handling not seeing her boyfriend. And she really was staying clean and sober; the regular drug testing was confirming it.

Everything seemed to be on track for reunification. One Saturday Emma even earned the privilege of having Hope all day at the beach with her family. Everyone was excited, and Hope returned to us tired but happy after having a good day.

Hope's behavior was slowly improving as well—something we were very thankful for. Doris and Russell were noticing the improvement too.

The following week at the courthouse, Doris and I were talking on a bench outside the courtroom. I asked her how the day at the beach had gone. Doris was reserved as she told me that Emma hadn't taken care of Hope the whole time but had left her with Emma's siblings while she played volleyball with friends. Doris also seemed disappointed as she shared that she'd found out that Emma had lied about her whereabouts recently.

Doris was grieved but not surprised by this, and she dutifully reported the developments to the social worker, which was really hard to do even though it was the right thing. Doris wanted the very best for Hope and loved both Emma and Hope too much to enable Emma's behavior. The social worker, a strong, no-nonsense woman, was concerned and said she'd look into it. I left court that day with a feeling that everything was about to unravel.

Doris called the next day with bombshell news. The police had arrested Emma for violating the no-contact court order. She had been seeing her boyfriend all along and lying to Doris. She was being kicked out of drug court and would need to start back at the beginning of the foster-care process to seek reunification with Hope.

Ugh! My heart fell.

Doris continued the story, telling me that the social worker had put an investigator on the case. The investigator found out that Emma had been lying and violating the court order. Emma was hysterical. She was frustrated that all these people in her life were telling her what to do, and she'd been crying to her mom about these awful new developments and their implications.

Doris had taken this as the opening she'd been praying for to discuss adoption with Emma. She encouraged Emma to think about what was best for Hope, which, Doris believed, would be to have John and me adopt her. It seemed that Emma had come to that conclusion herself. Though we'd thought this might happen all along, the fact that it was actually happening was hard to digest. I felt numb.

Doris told me I should expect a call from Emma.

I hung up and called John. Even though we'd anticipated this outcome, it didn't seem real. We were both in shock. We had been really cheering and praying for Emma to be able to parent Hope. John and I had mixed emotions. We wanted to adopt Hope, protect her, and raise her as our own, but we also wished that Emma was able to take care of her daughter.

"The other line is ringing. It's Emma; I have to go. I'll call you back," I hurriedly told John.

I clicked over to the other line. "Hello?"

"Auntie," said the familiar and sad voice of Emma.

"Hi, honey, are you okay?" I asked.

"Not really." She was crying. "Auntie, will you and uncle adopt Hope?"

"Yes, honey, we will," I assured her. "You know we're proud of you for getting off drugs, and we'll always pray for you and want the best for you."

"I know," she said, still crying. "I don't want Hope stuck in foster care for a long time. I remember how confusing that was for me when I was in foster care. I hated how short the visits were and the back and forth and all those people in my life. I just don't want that for her. I know you'll take good care of her," Emma continued.

"We will, sweetie," I promised her.

That was the essence of the call. It wasn't much longer than that because Emma was in an incredibly difficult place. She wanted everyone out of her life—no more social workers, guardians, drug-court people, judges. She wanted to do what she wanted with her boyfriend and not have anyone tell her otherwise.

I'm sorry to say that I think her decision to give her child up for adoption haunts her to this day, even though she knows it was the right thing to do.

John and I met with Emma after that to talk things through in person. She wanted to see Hope as often as she wanted, but we couldn't agree to that. All we could do was assure her that we would always act in what we believed was Hope's best interest and that we'd make sure to send pictures, updates, and so on. Emma agreed to our terms.

Now that we had Emma's agreement, we only needed to deal with the Bill situation. We honestly felt he would have his parental rights terminated because of his history. But, maddeningly, Emma's parents still couldn't get the police to do anything about Bill. He still hadn't been held accountable for his relationship with Emma. And not only that, child-welfare officials were now doing everything they could to reunite Hope with him.

Except for the age-of-consent issue, I'd had good relationships with local law-enforcement officials, having worked with them as a lobbyist on other issues, such as domestic violence, commercial sexual exploitation, and gambling. So I tried working my law-enforcement connections to get justice concerning Bill, but to no avail. No one would do anything.

I had one last call to make. It was pulling a major card. Back during the age-of-sexual consent battle, there was one really signifi-cant person who had been on our side. At the time, he was a lawyer in private practice who had waited for hours at the legislature to testify in support of raising the age of sexual consent. I didn't know him at the time, but I was so grateful to have him on our side. He seemed to be one of the only legal voices of reason at the time.

And now he was the attorney general of the state of Hawaii.

I called him and explained the situation. He was a fierce protector of children in all areas, but he was especially serious about protecting kids from sexual predators. He took this seriously and couldn't really understand why others didn't as well. In a highly unusual yet appropriate move, he assigned one of his own investigators to the case.

I was so grateful! It's impossible to put into words the relief I felt that the attorney general was involved. Each new day proved the critical nature of his involvement and brought a new level of attention from DHS, although the process was still shockingly slow.

Then, in the biggest stunner to that point, the attorney general's investigator uncovered that Bill had done jail time in another state for sexually molesting a young girl—his stepdaughter.

The smoking gun!

In spite of the fact that our social worker lacked this vital information, this bombshell didn't seem to faze DHS one bit. The agency told us it didn't officially matter. Bill had parental rights. He just needed a psychological exam to determine whether he was a fit parent.

We were furious. But we had to follow the process and be patient, knowing all the while that this could take years. It was demoralizing and maddening.

Around this same time, to our surprise, John and I began to sense that the Lord might be moving us off the island again. I had been discussing a potential job with Focus on the Family as the senior director of the Sanctity of Human Life department—right up my alley. Through my work with the Hawaii Family Forum, I'd been associated with Focus on the Family for nearly a decade and had many friends who worked there. The job possibility and the idea of moving back to the mainland were both intriguing.

The fact was that even though John and I had thought we'd live on the island the rest of our lives after we moved back, the cost of living in Hawaii was still outrageous, and our quickly growing family was making it difficult to make ends meet once again. The modest home we rented would have sold for $1.5 million, and a gallon of milk cost $7 at the time.

Our ongoing bonding difficulty with Joshua, combined with all the entanglements and people involved in the Hope situation, was wearing us down, and frankly, we wanted a fresh start. We wanted off the island.

But how will that work? we wondered.

Our longing to leave Hawaii and the new job opportunity seemed to coincide, but the Hope situation showed no signs of closure for a very long time.

To be perfectly honest, I'd suggested to John that we just move anyway. We had to think of what was best for our kids and our family, and we didn't want to pass up the chance to move back to the mainland through the job with Focus.

But even as I heard myself making that case, I knew it was just my way of having a tantrum. I wanted to be done with this hard stuff, and I wanted out. I knew it was wrong. John and I went back and forth about it.

"Let's just go," I would say.

"But we've made a commitment to helping Hope. What will happen to her? She needs us," John would answer patiently.

"Don't we have an obligation to do what's best for Daniel, Anna, and Joshua, and wouldn't that be moving to the mainland?" I countered, knowing all along that what I was saying was wrong and disobedient, however rational it sounded.

"But what has God called us to do?" John just kept responding, not pushing too hard. He always knew how to defuse me. It wasn't that I didn't want to adopt Hope; I was just tired of the struggle and wanted it to be behind us. Plain and simple. I guess in that way, I felt much like Emma had.

John and I prayed about the situation, and I eventually came to the conclusion John had already reached: We couldn't and wouldn't leave Hope. We'd stay in Hawaii for as long as it took to resolve things. We'd stay for Hope.

So I dove back in and lobbied hard for Hope. I had to make sure the out-of-state police and court reports about Bill's sexual-molestation conviction were faxed and sometimes refaxed to the social worker and the guardian. I had to make sure the judge was made aware of these developments and that everyone had the documentation they needed to support terminating Bill's parental rights.

I was more than happy to do it, of course. I relished the role, truth be told. God made me an advocate, and now I had the opportunity to be an advocate for my little girl. But it was ridiculous how hard I had to fight to make things right. The whole process was very frustrating.

In the meantime, things with Hope were improving. Her behavior was slowly getting under control, and she was using more appropriate language. Her sweet little voice brought joy to our days, and she clearly needed and loved us. The other kids were crazy about her, and she was already calling John and me "Dad" and "Mom." There were also some bright spots in the battle. The attorney general's investigator saw the risk Bill was to the community and to children, and she worked hard to see that justice was served.

Bill was and is an interesting character. Despite his actions, the truth of the matter is that he, too, was made in the image and likeness of almighty God and was in need of love and forgiveness. That was a hard fact to keep in mind at times, but John and I tried. As adoptive parents, we knew how important it was to remember that our children's birth parents were part of their pasts, and we needed to maintain a Christlike attitude toward them even if we disapproved of their harmful choices. It was no easy task and could only be accomplished by God's grace.

We knew we needed to protect Hope (and any other child) from Bill, but we also knew that it wasn't up to us to decide whether he was worthy of the same grace and mercy that we received from God. We didn't deserve God's grace any more than Bill did. John and I wrestled regularly with that truth.

We hired a child-welfare attorney, and he was expensive. My brother was kind enough to lend us some money, and we braced for a long, hard fight. John and I believed we'd prevail, but there was no telling how long it would take. A key court hearing was coming up, and our expensive lawyer told me not to say everything I wanted to say in the court report. He said it wouldn't be smart to show the judge we were against Bill getting his daughter back. He wanted us to just wait dispassionately until Bill's rights were terminated and then make it clear we wanted to adopt Hope.

I just couldn't do it. I disregarded his counsel and held nothing back, writing in the report that we believed Bill knew deep in his heart that Hope would be better off with us. We made it clear that if Bill allowed us to adopt Hope, we'd make sure she always knew he loved her as best he knew how. We contrasted her future with us and her siblings to her future with him. I appropriately reminded the court of Bill's criminal background and asked the judge to expedite Hope's future with us. We had her birth mother and grandparents all on our side, and she'd been with us for six months.

My lawyer said he wished I hadn't done that. And then came a bit of bad news. I found out that we were going to have a substitute judge for our hearing. My heart sank. Substitute judges generally won't do anything bold. This one would likely just set another review hearing in three to six months, even though he had my impassioned report asking him to expedite the process for Hope's sake.

John and I were frustrated. We wanted badly to move to the mainland, but we had decided to stay as long as necessary for Hope. It seemed we were in for a long, drawn-out process.

Late one morning, I called Doris to check in, just as I did five times a week. As usual, she had a million things going on and was trying to keep everything together, and I could hear it in her voice. But I heard something else, too. Some excitement.

"Oh, Kelly, I've been meaning to call you. Bill called me at eleven last night."

"What? Are you kidding? You meant to call me?" I couldn't believe she hadn't called me yet. "What did he say?" I asked impatiently.

"He got your court report, and he was crying. He said he wants what's best for Hope, and he'll let you adopt her, but he wants to talk to you first. You need to call him right away."

I was shaking.

I hung up the phone and called John to tell him that it was possible our prayers were being answered. Neither of us could believe it. We had resigned ourselves to the long fight, and this seemed too good to be true. I had to hang up quickly so I could call Bill.

I dialed his number and felt sick to my stomach. I was uttering prayers under my breath—*Please, please, God.*

Bill answered the phone. As nervous as I was, he seemed much more so. And he was upset. He said he didn't know our other children had been adopted, and he didn't know we wanted to adopt Hope.

I didn't know whether that was true, since Bill was one of the best manipulators we'd ever met, but we agreed that John and I should meet with him that evening—face-to-face. We set the time and location, telling him we'd come anywhere he wanted at any time. The meeting was to be at six o'clock over the mountain in Kailua Town. John and I arranged for a babysitter to watch the kids and nervously began that drive over the mountain. A million things had been going through my mind, including whether we should take along my six-foot-four ex-NFL-lineman dad for protection, considering Bill's instability.

The adrenaline I was experiencing was beyond description. Excitement, fear, dread, anxiety, nausea . . . hope. John and I couldn't wait to get there, yet we were both afraid to arrive. Might this nightmare finally be over? Could this long ordeal really be coming to an end? Could we finally rest easy knowing that Hope's future with us was secure? It seemed too good to be true; it was such a crazy turn of events.

We pulled up to the restaurant and saw Bill sitting alone at a tiny table outside. He stood up when we arrived. We shook hands and sat down. Bill was visibly upset, and John and I (amazingly!) both felt great compassion for him. Bill clearly loved Hope in his own way, and this was agonizing for him. As he talked, it was obvious that he wanted what was best for Hope.

John and I were attentive listeners, not wanting to cause any problems by being confrontational. We let Bill talk. And he talked a lot. He tried to convince us that he was wrongly convicted on the child-molestation offense in the other state. He cried as he sadly and rather bizarrely told us how he knew from the beginning that fourteen-year-old Emma was going to break his heart. This poor man had serious issues.

He told us about his horrible childhood. Though it wasn't hard to believe that he had a bad childhood, we really had no idea what to believe because he was such a cunning manipulator. Even so, we still felt sorry for him.

After Bill had talked a good long time, we assured him that Hope would always know he loved her and that he chose to put her interests above his own. We praised him for being selfless in looking out for her, not himself. We spoke to him about the love of a God who forgives our sins through faith in Christ. He seemed to be a broken man.

We were honest and told him we were concerned that he'd change his mind and string us along. Bill assured us that he was a man of his word. Of course, that meant nothing to us, but he seemed resolute, and we left that night with his assurance that this would be a done deal. He said he would consent to Hope's adoption.

Cautiously optimistic . . . you're probably familiar with the phrase. Politicians use it when they are up in the polls but the votes haven't been counted yet.

Well, we were cautiously optimistic, hoping we could trust Bill to keep his word. But in the world of adoption, nothing is final until it's *final.* Bill certainly didn't have a good track record, but this was a great development. After our meeting, I got busy working the phones. I called the social worker with the joyous news. She didn't act joyous. She would need to independently verify this. I called the guardian and told her. Same reaction.

Apparently, I had really annoyed all these people with my, um, advocacy. I saw it as necessary; they saw it as a bother, a major pain in the neck. To me, it's one of the terrible aspects of the system. The more you advocate for your child, the more you risk getting a bad rap. If you keep quiet and just house kids, sometimes it goes better for you. I found that extremely frustrating.

But regardless, as we'd done so often over the past several years, John and I continued to pray hard, and I lobbied our case to the best of my ability. I stayed in constant touch with Bill to encourage him and make sure he did what he needed to for the adoption to take place. I wanted to keep checking in with him to confirm that he wasn't going to change his mind.

He told me that people all throughout the system had tried to talk him into changing his mind. He said he'd been told he should fight for Hope and not let us adopt her. I didn't and still don't know whether that was true. Sadly, I can believe it.

One day as we neared the official hearing for Bill to relinquish his parental rights, my phone rang. It was a man who identified himself as Bill's coworker. He told me he was a Christian and had been talking to Bill for a long time about doing what was right for Hope and letting us adopt her. I marveled at the way the Lord had been answering our prayers during this process, even through the actions of a total stranger.

He told me to keep fighting for Hope, but he also shared with me his fear that Bill was suicidal. He was Bill's friend, trying to save his life and lead him to Christ. And God had used him to help convince Bill to do what was best for Hope.

What I knew at the time that Bill didn't know was that he was still likely to be arrested for his conduct with Emma. Bill's coworker seemed to understand this was possible but didn't want Bill to know for fear that he'd take his life. The coworker thought he'd been able to talk Bill out of any suicidal thoughts, but he didn't want any other news to push him back the other way. I thanked him for the call, and then I called John. Later that night, we prayed for Bill.

Thankfully, Bill seemed to stabilize, and the day came for the court ruling on terminating his parental rights. We were terrified he would show up and announce that he'd changed his mind. But as we sat in court that day, we watched Bill fulfill his commitment. He read something aloud that he had written about how Hope had been a joy to him and now she would be to us. The judge commended him for his decision not to stand in the way of Hope's adoption and told him it was the right thing for him to do. His parental rights were terminated that day. He was later prosecuted and served time in jail.

In the foster-care adoption process, the point at which the birth parents' rights are legally terminated is hugely significant. Before that happens, birth parents have significant rights, and foster parents have virtually none. After parental rights are terminated, there is a tad more breathing room for the foster parents. It's always a bittersweet thing. There is sadness over the loss of what should have been. But there is also great joy if it means a child is now free to enjoy a life without abuse and neglect.

And just like that, we were on the homestretch to finalize Hope's adoption.

22

Blue Cotton Candy

I mentioned earlier that I knew and had worked with the top DHS officials in Hawaii. The Hawaii Family Forum had partnered with Deeanna's Christian adoption agency, HOPE In the Name of Christ (HOPE INC), and DHS to help raise awareness of and recruit adoptive families for Hawaii's waiting kids in foster care. In my role as director of HFF, I spoke in churches, getting the word out and connecting families to HOPE INC.

Another of my roles that year was to coordinate and emcee the national adoption celebration for the whole state of Hawaii. Each year during this celebration, the courthouse opens on Saturday, and many adoptions from foster care are finalized on the same day in a group celebration.

This year was to be no exception, and after the finalizations, we would have a celebration on the courthouse steps. I would not only coordinate and emcee the event but also do media interviews before and during the celebration. It was one of the best parts of my job, spreading awareness about the blessing of adoption.

While preparing for this event, I had the opportunity via e-mail to tell a colleague, who was a DHS official, about the fact that Bill had relinquished his parental rights so we could adopt Hope. She broached the idea of finalizing Hope's adoption on National Adoption Day, November 17, 2007, as part of the big celebration. Makes sense, you might think. But National Adoption Day was only three weeks away, and adoption finalizations *never*, and I mean *never*, happen that fast. I had been thinking and scheming and hoping for such a thing but hadn't dared mention it for fear of backlash from the social worker.

The DHS official's suggestion was all I needed to try to move forward. I wish I could adequately describe all the unbelievable things that occurred to make this a reality. Of course, it was all God's amazing grace and guiding hand. But He used almost ten years' worth of relationships in government to help make it happen. A litany of judges and other state employees were so kind in making it happen; it nearly takes my breath away remembering it.

About a week before the big day, our family was chosen to be the adoptive family the lieutenant governor would honor in the governor's conference room at the National Adoption Day Proclamation event. The kids got dressed up and looked darling in their special outfits. It was a great celebration.

One exception after another was made for us, and it was starting to look as if our dream might come true: We would be finalizing Hope's adoption on Hawaii's National Adoption Day at an event I would be emceeing.

It doesn't get much more special than that.

The day of the event was a perfect Hawaiian day—warm breezes, gorgeous blue skies, and for John and me, a sense of joy and relief. Our four kids were dressed in their fancy clothes, each with a Hawaiian lei around their necks, of course. Daniel was seven, Anna was six, Joshua was five, and Hope was three. It had been seven years since we had first started this adoption journey. What an adventure it had been.

We arrived early with all the other families and went through the official adoption finalization inside the courthouse. Once all the families were finished, the judges, who volunteered their time that day, all lined up outside in their robes as the new adoptive families gathered round.

I then had the great privilege of leading a group-adoption-finalization reenactment for the media, and then we had a grand celebration. There were booths for the kids to get stickers, face painting, and balloons, and great food abounded for young and old. Friends from church came out to support us, including Uncle Pastor Chris.

John and I will never forget the sight of our four children running and playing with huge smiles and gigantic cones of blue cotton candy. It was amazing to us that we were now a family of six. We were still in awe at how God had worked out the details for Hope's adoption on this day. We were so relieved, so excited for the future, and so tired. Truly, we were completely and utterly exhausted, but we were happy.

We had our customary post-adoption meal at a nice restaurant with my family. After lunch we went home and napped, finally sleeping with a peace we hadn't had for some time.

23

Aloha Hawaii or Colorado Bound

The process of getting hired by Focus on the Family was a roller-coaster ride. I had met Focus on the Family's vice president of the Sanctity of Human Life department, Yvette Maher, and, well, if I can say it without sounding odd, I just fell in love.

Yvette was and is one of the most amazing people I've ever had the pleasure to know. We met because of Focus on the Family's How to Drug Proof Your Kids program, which Yvette and her team at Focus had brought to Hawaii. The Hawaii Family Forum hosted the event at a church and included leaders of Hawaii's drug-abuse prevention community. Yvette and I hit it off right away.

I confided to her that John and I were thinking about moving back to the U.S. mainland, and at that time Yvette had indicated that she might have an open position in her department.

The thought *I could work for her* ran through my mind.

John really wanted to get off the rock, as they say in Hawaii. He was weary in his job and was concerned about the cost of living and our future now that we had four kids. Now that things were settled with Hope's adoption, John was actually the biggest proponent of our moving back to the mainland. We were feeling frazzled and wanted a fresh start.

My mother and her husband, along with my brother and his family, lived in Colorado, and we loved it there. So moving to Colorado Springs seemed ideal for us.

John and I were really excited about this possibility, but it was taking so long. First, there was the delay on our end because of the Hope situation, but then, just when the adoption was finalized and things seemed clear on our end, everything seemed to slow down on the Focus end.

Frustration. We were discouraged.

But we really tried to practice regularly giving the uncertainty and the future to God. After all, what else could we do? It's not as if we were these superspiritual people by any stretch, but we had no other choice than to continue learning in a deeper way how to accept that God was in control, not us. We thought we'd move to Colorado, and I'd work at Focus and John would enjoy his post–air force retirement time as a stay-at-home dad, something he really longed to do.

We had both wanted me to be home while the kids were little. We never knew how that would be possible with my school debt, but the Lord made a way for it to happen. I worked part-time from home when the kids were very young, but now that they were in preschool and elementary school, John and I both really wanted to structure things so that he could stay home with them. We know that's not for everyone, but we both believed it was the way the Lord was leading us.

Yvette and I communicated back and forth, but the wait was always "just a little bit longer."

At one point, I hadn't heard from Focus in a while, so I placed several calls to Yvette. She never called back. "It must have fallen through," I told John. "She's not returning my calls anymore." It seemed so strange to me, so unlike Yvette and so opposite of where we thought God was leading.

What once seemed like a near certainty now seemed impossible. I was trying to accept that the job at Focus just wasn't going to happen. It was hard to wrap my brain around this because I had felt so sure it was where God wanted me. Had we missed God's leading in this? John and I wondered aloud to each other.

In the meantime, the governor of Hawaii had just appointed me to be the chairperson of a newly created Family Celebration Commission. I was at the state capitol getting ready to chair a meeting in the governor's conference room when my cell phone rang, showing a call from the Colorado Springs area code.

"Hello," I answered, excited but trying not to get my hopes up.

"Kelly? Kelly, is it really you?"

It was Yvette. My heart leaped. I can still remember leaning over the fifth-floor balcony of the gorgeous state capitol building, staring at the ocean as she talked.

"I've been calling you back at the wrong number." She laughed loudly, and we picked right up where we'd left off, planning the next steps for my prospective job at Focus.

Yvette explained that she still wanted me to be the senior director of the Sanctity of Human Life department. She explained the budget, timing, and approval process. She would know soon if everything was approved, and then she would contact me. She felt confident but made clear that nothing was ever final until it was *final* at Focus on the Family. God had sure prepared us through adoption for that reality.

Yvette wanted me to begin thinking about when we could move. The timing would be tricky because the Hawaii legislature would begin another legislative session in January, and I had to get the Hawaii Family Forum through the busiest first few months. Yvette and I agreed to pray and stay in close touch during the next steps. We e-mailed often, and John and I were gleeful, thinking about a fresh start for our future.

When that conversation with Yvette ended, I called John and told him the great news. Then I walked into the governor's conference room with a strange realization in my heart that our time in this place that had been such a huge part of our lives for almost ten years was really and truly coming to an end.

Focus arranged for me to fly to Colorado Springs for an interview. I was able to stay with my dear friend Martha from Hawaii, who now lived in Colorado Springs, and by the end of the three days, I had an offer to work at Focus on the Family. My mom and family were thrilled, and so were John and I.

We had used the Internet to research possible houses for purchase, and I planned to visit the top five while I was in Colorado. Our favorite house on the Internet was hands down the best house I saw. Housing in Colorado was roughly one-third the price of housing in Hawaii. So we were able to buy a home with plenty of space and a big yard for the kids to play in. Those amenities are out of reach for most people in Hawaii.

We were moving to Colorado. It was really happening! We'd be able to spend holidays with my family and be closer to John's family. We were really thrilled. But at the same time, we were sad to be leaving dear friends and family in Hawaii. My dad and siblings were still there. And we loved and adored so many friends from Kaimuki Christian Church and the Hawaii Family Forum, who had been like family to us for nearly a decade. That part was very sad for us.

God had changed our lives radically since He had first brought us to Hawaii. He'd given us our children and dramatically deepened our faith. We had glorious and bittersweet going away parties at church and HFF. The HFF board of directors and my colleague Eva were like family to me. I always believed the work at HFF was part of why I was put on this earth. It was tough to leave those people we loved.

John and I will never forget our last Sunday at Kaimuki Christian Church. I wept as I considered all God had done in our lives through this wonderful church and its dear, loving people. We'd worshipped and served together. We'd taught Sunday school for their preschoolers; we'd enjoyed meals together and worked alongside each other to reach our community for Christ. Folks had prayed for us regularly, brought meals, and babysat the kids. Our church family loved us well. Saying good-bye to our friends and family was a difficult point in an otherwise very exciting time.

24

Rocky Mountain Challenge

Our arrival on the U.S. mainland marked the ending of a significant chapter in our lives. Whew . . . what a ride it had been! We were finally on our way to the beginning of the rest of our story, living happily ever after.

We settled into our new house. All the space was a dream. Hawaii houses were so close together that our neighbors once called the police on us because of Hope's screaming. We were pinching ourselves in disbelief over our great life on the mainland. We found a wonderful church. I loved my job at Focus. John loved being a stay-at-home dad, and he began studying for a master's degree online. The kids enjoyed their new school and being closer to Grandma, Papa, and other extended family.

The kids also loved Colorado winters with school cancellations, sledding, snowball fights, and plenty of hot chocolate by a roaring fireplace. And John and the kids finally got their wish—a dog! A magnificent, wonderful, cute, adorable Labradoodle puppy we named Koa, which means "warrior" in Hawaiian. Later, we would get a second little Labradoodle puppy and name her Lady.

If you're not a dog person, you won't get this, but Koa and Lady have brought an indescribable amount of love and joy to our family. We love our doodles. I wasn't a dog person until these two came along. I'm now fully in the dog-person camp. And John, well, you've never seen a man love his dogs the way John loves Koa and Lady.

All of our children have or have had some type of special need. Daniel has Tourette's syndrome, attention deficit disorder (ADD), and asthma; Joshua had severe developmental delays from his difficult start; and Hope had some developmental delays too, along with behavioral challenges that often got her into trouble at school. Anna was diagnosed with asthma and suffered several serious and scary bouts of the croup that led to her throat nearly closing up. Between Daniel and Anna, we've seen our fair share of emergency rooms for terrifying breathing difficulties. Small children and breathing problems are a really scary combination.

About a year after we arrived in Colorado, one of our children started to display some severe behavioral changes. I'm sure you can appreciate why we want to keep the child's identity private. But for storytelling purposes, we'll say it was one of the girls.

She developed a much shorter fuse. She would get angry and then lose all her usual logic skills. John and I couldn't reason with her. The only thing that would restore her to her usual self was time. She would go to her room and emerge, back to normal, after a while.

We didn't think too much about it at first. But soon, whenever she didn't get what she wanted, she would wail and rage for hours at a time. She would scratch John and me to the point of drawing blood. She would scratch herself, throw things, hit us, break things, and leave the house, threatening to run away. She spewed awful words at us—previously unthinkable things—such as she hated us, wished she'd never been born, didn't want to be alive, and so on.

John and I did all the usual parenting stuff, including threatening severe consequences if she didn't shape up. Nothing worked. I mean, *nothing worked*. This continued to happen with increasing frequency.

John and I cried out to God for insight and help. These rages seemed beyond her control. Yet her actions were so violent, her screaming so full of vitriol, each episode lasting for hours, that we were soon living in perpetual terror and exhaustion. And to make things worse, her behavior toward the other kids was becoming really horrible.

She begged us to homeschool her, and John was able to do that, which made her somewhat less anxious. We sought professional help from a counselor who worked with a lot of adopted kids who'd come from difficult backgrounds and experienced serious challenges. She told us our experience was normal, though in most cases the challenges arise shortly after the child is adopted, not years later, as in our case.

At the end of one episode of rage, our daughter said she didn't trust herself. From what she told us, it seemed that even when she knew something, she felt she had to add "I think" as a qualifier whenever she responded to us.

For example, I would ask, "Honey, did you throw your cup away?"

"Yes," she would say, "I think I did," even if she had just done it moments before.

John and I had noticed that she started doing this right around the time of her first rage episode. She also said she didn't like to read anymore because she had to keep rereading the pages because she didn't trust that she'd already read them.

This experience cemented in our minds what we knew in our

hearts—this wasn't our child's fault. It wasn't about her behavior or consequences or discipline issues. Something was wrong, and we needed to figure out what it was.

Some time later, when I mentioned to my team at work about my daughter rereading things and not trusting herself, my friend Amanda came to life, explaining that this was just what her sister had experienced growing up. Amanda went on to describe how hard it was for her as the sibling, but how God had helped her sister through medication. Her sister was now in college and doing well. It gave me great hope. Amanda was kind enough to come to the house that day and talk to our family about how hard it was for her as the sibling. Her words, like those of our therapist, confirmed that our daughter was sick and not simply misbehaving.

So our next stop was a pediatric behavioral specialist. She diagnosed generalized anxiety disorder and obsessive-compulsive tendencies. OCD—that made sense. Our daughter would get fixated on something and would literally seem unable to get the thought out of her head.

The supposed cure was an anti-anxiety drug, and it seemed to help for a while. But then our daughter regressed, and the frequency and intensity of her rages grew worse than ever. She didn't want to take her meds, and life was a constant battle. The doctor wanted us to try slightly different doses and give the medication much more time to work. John and I felt we didn't have much left before we cracked.

One night in August 2010, almost a year after the rages had begun, I talked for a long time with a good friend, Gloria. She had adopted children out of foster care who, because of early trauma, had acted out even worse than our daughter. One of her sons, Tim, had been so violent that she'd had to call the police on numerous occasions. I had seen her take Tim to every kind of therapist, try every possible medicine, use every parenting tool and behavioral intervention, and recruit many people to pray for him. Nothing had ever worked.

Now, however, Gloria was telling me that Tim hadn't had a rage episode in two full months. I couldn't believe my ears. "What did you do?" I asked.

"We learned through Texas Christian University's Institute for Child Development that we should have Tim's neurotransmitter levels tested to find out if he has an imbalance in his brain," she told me excitedly. "His levels were totally out of balance. We put him on the prescribed supplements, and, Kelly, his raging has virtually stopped."

I felt hope rise in me. If Tim could get better, so could our daughter. Gloria explained how to find the right kind of doctor in my area to get the testing. She told me this treatment was seen as nontraditional and that some doctors might be unfamiliar with it.

This dear friend had tried to tell me about the therapy months earlier, but it had seemed to me like just the latest fad. Gloria hadn't yet had success with Tim back then, so she was just sharing what she'd been learning and felt excited about. I hadn't paid much attention. But the proof for me was Tim's improvement. Now I was all ears.

With help from my friend Yvette, we found a doctor in our area, and I made an appointment, but it wouldn't be for another several weeks. Meanwhile, our daughter's rages continued, and for the first time in our nearly twenty-year marriage, John and I were losing patience with each other. The other kids started acting out.

During this period, I tried to throw myself into God. I wanted to learn how to be at peace in the Lord, even if my daughter's circumstances never changed. I tried to want that more than I wanted things to change. I wanted to learn to praise God right in the midst of the hardest times. But at the same time, I was in despair. I wanted the girl I knew back in our lives.

God was our rock and our fortress through this time; He truly was and is "an ever-present help" in time of need (Psalm 46:1). And, oh, did we need Him. We were upheld by the faithful prayers of our friends—Amy, Justine, Debi, Yvette, Martha, Carrie, Natalie, Kirsten, and others. I would text them as soon as an episode started, and they covered us in prayer. I'm grateful they never seemed to tire of my SOS prayer texts.

Even in those dark times, there were small moments of hope. For example, God used the trials with his sister to make Daniel a shockingly patient child who regularly considers the needs of others above his own. And there is no feeling like seeing our children advocate for one another and demonstrate great compassion and kindness when one of their siblings has a challenge.

It's hard to explain, but God provided John and me with just enough strength for each day, even when getting through the day didn't seem possible. During our darkest times of crying out to God, there always seemed to be a brief respite; our daughter's behavior would stabilize for the night or for a few hours. The respites were few but enough to remind us that God was with us and truly wouldn't give us more than we could handle. Faithful friends were also praying for us regularly and were always ready to listen and encourage. Their support helped keep us going.

The day of the doctor's appointment finally came. A simple urine test was performed at the office and then our daughter had to do a saliva test throughout the day with a home kit. John filled out lots of paperwork. Then we waited another six tough weeks for the results.

When we saw the doctor again, he walked into the room, read the report, and said slowly, "Well, I'm surprised her feet are even on the ground."

Hallelujah! I thought. *There's something wrong.*

"They're not often on the ground—she's usually on her head or doing flips," I quipped.

The doctor showed us the lab results, which identified what normal levels of ten neurotransmitters should look like. And then he showed us her levels. Half of them were literally off the charts, and the other half were dramatically above normal ranges.

The doctor calmly summed up the results with this remark: "Her levels are like gasoline on fire."

John and I could have cried with joy. Yes, gasoline on fire . . . explosive; that's what our daughter was like. It was a perfect description. We weren't going crazy.

The doctor explained his treatment recommendations to help balance her out. And just as Gloria had told me, it was simple supplements. He recommended three different kinds.

I'll never forget the feeling of hope I had as we left the office that day, hope that we had found the answer. I also remember feeling a cautionary check in my gut that I promptly ignored. I couldn't face the reality that we might have to deal with more of what we'd been going through.

I would like to say that this new course of treatment brought an end to our daughter's episodes, and that she is now completely free of her affliction. But that wouldn't be true. About a week after she started the supplement regimen, she had horrible, violent episodes three days in a row. Yet we survived that stretch, and shortly afterward, we enjoyed more than three weeks without an episode. Amazing!

John and I knew better than to get our hopes too high, though. And about a month into this new treatment, her episodes returned to their previous frequency. But on the positive side, for the first time ever, they started to lessen in intensity and length. The improvement was enough to refresh our hope.

Ups and downs, that's where we lived at the time—and it's where we live now. When her episodes occur, they can be quite scary. She's still a recluse who doesn't often want to leave the house. And she has a hard time being away from either John or me, for the most part.

As is common with chronic illness, for a while we kept trying to adjust her supplements, hoping to find just the right dosage for her specific symptoms. We finally stumbled upon a combination that really seemed to improve things. Again, we went one, two, three, four weeks without any episodes. We saw a return of courtesy, joy, and a tolerance for the word *no*. Serious progress.

Now our daughter's happy again. Her beautiful smile appears more easily and more often. She laughs and jokes. She can actually stand to be in the same room with her siblings and even plays joyfully again with them at times. As we've gone through this difficult experience, John and I have reminded each other constantly that even if she never gets any better than she is now, we can handle it by God's grace.

Even with the progress we've seen, there is no neat and tidy ending to the challenges we face with our daughter. No perfect, pretty bows. But there is God's grace and faithfulness in the midst of our messiness, failures, and brokenness. There is perseverance and hope in Christ. There is deep peace and even joy. There is amazing love. We love our daughter so much. There is reaching out to help others who need the comfort God has given us.

And there is this truth: We would never want to experience life without our daughter or any of our kids—whether that means life is easy or difficult. After all, where did we get the notion that the Christian life would be trouble-free? That's not what Christ promised us. But He did promise that He would be with us in the midst of everything. He has promised that in the end, we will overcome just as He has. He has promised that He loves each precious human being made in His image and likeness. And He calls His followers to reflect that same kind of love.

Recently I was talking with our ill child about how much we love being her mommy and daddy and how thankful we are that God made us a family through adoption.

"Mom . . ." she said very thoughtfully, and then there was a long pause. "Would you still have fought to adopt me if you'd known then about what's been happening lately . . . about, um, you know?"

We all want desperately to be wanted, don't we?

She wanted to know if she was worth it. She needed to know whether all the problems made her any less desirable or lovable. She needed to hear again that John and I love her unconditionally.

It was an amazing moment.

"Honey, of course, we would have fought just as hard for you," I said stroking her beautiful cheeks. "There's nothing you could ever do to lessen our love for you."

She beamed and moved on to the next thing, but she seemed a little more secure, maybe a little more healed.

And it occurred to me: That's what it all comes down to. She's worth it. Each of our children is worth it. We love them desperately and couldn't be more blessed.

Our children, like all children, are gifts from God. Daniel is one of the most kind and compassionate kids ever. Anna Grace is feisty and strong and has a heart for justice. Joshua is our easygoing boy with a beautiful smile who loves to be helpful. Our little Hope is a pistol who can charm anyone she meets. She's determined and strong-willed; only in Anna has she met her match.

Through our struggles, our kids have learned compassion, teamwork, and the reality of walking out the biblical admonition to "consider others better than yourselves" (Philippians 2:3). Even at such young ages, our kids demonstrate these characteristics in more ways than many adults I know. We might have preferred a different route to get where we are now, but that's God's business, not ours. He knows best, and we trust Him.

John and I have worked hard to create a sense of unity in our family. We call ourselves Team Rosati, and we constantly remind each other that even in the difficult times, nothing can ever stop our love for each other—and nothing can ever stop God's love for us. Our children have become fierce advocates for one another, and it's a beautiful thing to behold. They fight like all kids do, but they are also there for each other in ways that are beyond their years.

There have been countless magical moments of joy and laughter in addition to the heartaches and trials. We have lots of favorite family traditions and activities: saying our blessings each night around the dinner table; family movie nights with popcorn and soda; family devotions where the kids take turns reading the Scripture verses and leading us in prayer; and lots of hugs and kisses. We have so much joy and fun in our family, and our hearts swell whenever we think about our abundant blessings. We're far from being a perfect family, but that's okay—there are no perfect families.

Like all families, we have yelling, fighting, hurt feelings, messy rooms, and other aspects of a normal family life. But above all, we desire to be a family centered on God, fierce in our commitment to Him and to each other. One favorite moment for John and me is whenever we pull into the driveway and see all four of our kids laughing and playing with the Labradoodles in the yard. There's just something so beautiful about knowing we're a family and knowing that God knit us together.

We recently asked our children what our family means to them, and the following is just a sampling of how they responded.

Our precious eleven-year-old Daniel, who started his life detoxing from the drugs and alcohol his birth mother took during her pregnancy, said, "My family means we care about each other. When I need something or I'm hurt, they are always there for me. I have someone to go to when I'm sad, and someone to tell about my day at school." Our lovely nine-year-old daughter Anna expressed that she likes "the support and the fun. Dad's dancing is funny. The love is really good."

Our sweet Joshua, who barely talked when he first came home, is eight now and loves bugs, his dogs, and the great outdoors. He said, "Family is a whole bunch of people caring for you—loving you and stuff like that. They always stick up for each other." He expressed sadness for kids who don't have families because "it takes too long to get them families. . . . They have to wait too long."

Our little Hope is six years old. When asked what she likes about her family, she said, "I love the loving. . . . My sister is kind when I'm sad, and I like having brothers and a sister to play with."

John loves the sense of teamwork and the companionship. He loves the simplicity of just doing life together—whether he's belting out eighties Christian music as the kids roll their eyes or calling everyone around the computer, forcing them to watch the "Danke Schoen" YouTube video by Wayne Newton.

Before I had kids, I always thought how wonderful it would be to be that one person a child wants and needs more than any other human on earth. I love that. I love that when my kids cry, I can hold them and make it better even while the tears keep rolling. I love talking with them about the stuff of life—friends on the playground, personal interactions, confronting fear, opportunities to forgive or to seek wisdom from God. Seeing their spiritual growth is the most exciting and rewarding thing in life. Watching them grow in their understanding and experience of God's love thrills my soul.

Daniel recently shared with me that he felt God's leading during one of his quiet times about "fearing not" because God was with him. There is no happier feeling than to see your child walk with God.

And adoption made all of this possible for our family.

You see, John and I have learned that God's plan for us through adoption was even better than we could have imagined. We've learned personally about God's faithfulness through the dark times. We know He'll be there no matter what else comes our way. What a gift that is!

We want to encourage folks who are feeling that urge, that gentle pushing of the Lord's hand at your back, to get involved with foster care or adoption. Don't be afraid to go for it. There could be a child out there who needs you desperately. You could make a difference in his or her life. God may have a new adventure in store for your family. Be open. Follow where God leads.

25

Wait No More

I sometimes wonder about what might have happened to our children if God hadn't made us a family. It's hard to think about. Who would have held them when they cried? Who would have taken them to their seemingly endless doctor's appointments? Who would have made sure they got the special help and testing they've needed in school? Who would have played catch with them or H-O-R-S-E on the basketball court? Who would have played dolls with them or shown them how to use an Easy-Bake Oven? Who would have snuggled with them and prayed for them and sung to them?

These questions lead me inevitably to think about all the children out there, right this moment, who are still waiting for a place to call home, for caring people to be their family. For John and me, that thought makes our hearts hurt, and we want everyone to know about the blessing of adoption. It is our prayer that those waiting children will wait no more for the adoptive families they deserve, and that their prospective families will wait no more to begin the spiritual adventure of a lifetime.

It was out of this deep passion and desire to help those waiting children that Focus on the Family's Wait No More adoption initiative came into being. What an incredible blessing to be able to work in one's area of passion. Before I came to Focus, I had heard great things about the new president of Focus on the Family, Jim Daly. When I arrived, I wasn't disappointed. Jim has a huge heart. He's funny, passionate about Christ and families, and has an unrelenting commitment to orphan care and adoption.

Orphaned as a child, Jim knows the loneliness and pain of the kids in foster care awaiting adoption. He wanted our orphan-care work to flourish and gave the green light to make it happen. As the senior director of the Sanctity of Human Life department at Focus on the Family, I was privileged to be involved in founding our Wait No More program.

The program is based on the experiences John and I had in Hawaii, where we'd seen up close what could be accomplished when the state and the faith community worked together for the good of waiting children in foster care. But I knew we'd need a willing partner at the state level in Colorado. Thankfully, Yvette Maher and the other leaders at Focus gave us free rein to move ahead with this plan.

Through Wait No More, Focus on the Family partners with local child-welfare officials, churches, and adoption-agency leaders to recruit Christian families to adopt legal orphans trapped in foster care. In the United States, there are approximately 114,000 kids waiting for families and more than 300,000 churches. If only one family in every other church would adopt a waiting child, we could eliminate the list of waiting children.

With a biblical mandate to care for these children, there's no reason why all these waiting children can't get the families they deserve. This is the heart and charge of Jim Daly, the calling on my life, and the mission of Focus on the Family's Wait No More program.

We began Wait No More by partnering with Colorado's Department of Human Services under the incredible leadership of Dr.
Sharen Ford, the manager of the permanency unit. Dr. Ford has
spent more than twenty years advocating for kids in foster care. Her
passion is unending, and her commitment is relentless. She had already begun to make great progress helping Colorado's kids in foster care find adoptive families through key partnerships with the
faith-based community, including Christian ministries such as Project 1.27 in Denver. Together, we worked with many great adoption
agencies, counties, churches, and ministries.

Thanks to the incredible vision and heart of Pastor Brady Boyd,
we held our first Wait No More event at New Life Church in the
fall of 2008. Before we planned the event, I asked Dr. Ford what
she would think if 500 people attended and 100 families started the
process of foster-care adoption.

"Would that be considered a success?" I asked her in a DHS
conference room.

"Success times three," she answered.

"We could do this!" we said to each other.

It was an invigorating time. I remember driving south on I-25
along the Rocky Mountains, my heart soaring because I just knew
God was going to do a great thing for Colorado's kids in foster care.

When the event came, the Lord did exceedingly more than we
could have asked or hoped for. We had more than 1,300 people
show up that Saturday to learn about the needs of Colorado's waiting kids. And by the end of the day, more than 265 families had
started the process of adopting through foster care.

All the glory goes to God and God alone. I firmly believe it is
His heart, passion, and love for these kids that moves people's hearts.
After all, Scripture says that He is a "father to the fatherless" and

"sets the lonely in families" (Psalm 68:5, 6). It was and continues to be a privilege for me to be part of this program.

In fact, just two years after our first event, we'd seen almost 1,500 families in eight states across the U.S. start the foster-care adoption process. Throughout the country, 5,800 people representing 3,200 families and 1,400 churches have come out to learn about the needs of orphans in foster care.

Although we're a long way from achieving our goal of finding adoptive homes for all the waiting kids in the United States, God has worked through Wait No More to make great progress in this area.

The statistics, of course, never quite capture the whole picture. I never tire of hearing the homecoming stories we receive from adoptive families. One of my favorites is the Fosters' story (their name has been changed to protect their identity). The Fosters attended the first Wait No More event in Colorado and adopted a sibling group of four boys, ages three to seven. Those boys had been in foster care for years, and few people in the system held out hope that they would be able to place all the boys in one adoptive family.

The Fosters were a great Christian family with older birth kids. Their hearts were broken, as the Father's heart is, at the plight of kids in foster care who are awaiting adoption. But the family wanted to do more than simply feel badly; they wanted God to use them. So they walked forward in faith and adopted these four brothers. The Fosters' lives are busy and crazy, but the family says they are blessed "beyond anything we ever imagined."

Another family comes to mind—the Westees. They adopted two little girls after Wait No More and are now in the process of adopting two boys. They felt compelled to take action. A pastor and his wife in Missouri adopted teenage boys. It rocked their world. I'll never forget when the pastor described to me that going through the adoption process was like "pouring Miracle-Gro on your sin." I laughed out loud. It's so true. So much of this process is about God changing and growing us—the parents—to be more like Christ. It's painful sometimes, but the heart of the Christian life is to be transformed and become more like Christ.

Tiffany Beal, a speaker for Wait No More, has one of the most powerful testimonies you'll ever hear. She and her siblings entered foster care after their youngest sibling died from neglect. Tiffany was told that she was too old to be adopted, and she certainly wouldn't be adopted with her siblings. Thankfully, nothing is impossible with God, and a wonderful Christian family adopted eleven-year-old Tiffany, along with her two younger siblings. She had much healing to do, but her family loved her unconditionally and never gave up on her.

Today, she is twenty, married, and blessing others as a nurse with a particular passion for new moms and their babies. She is a living, breathing testimony to the unending grace and unconditional love of our all-powerful God.

I did an interview with a reporter a few months back. I explained the Wait No More program to her and told her that prospective adoptive families are educated extensively about the challenges they may face, and yet they are inspired to act as they hear about the needs of the children and God's heart for them. I'll never forget her response: "You mean Christian couples are learning how hard this might be, and in the end they are still doing it anyway because it's the heart of God?" Precisely. That's it.

If every Christian family in the United States would simply commit to pray and ask God if *He* wants to use them to bless a child without a family, well, we'd change the world. If we can get the church to think about adoption not in terms of the desires of adults but in terms of the needs of children, I think we'd see on a much grander scale how God sets the lonely in families.

Another part of Wait No More is helping the church understand that although not everyone is called to adopt, everyone is called to do something on behalf of orphans. And one critically important thing we need the church to do is support the adoptive families in their congregations.

We want to do all we can through the Wait No More program to let churches know about the spiritual and practical needs of adoptive families in their congregations and equip them to effectively come alongside and walk this journey with them. When you parent "kids from hard places," as one expert calls them, you face challenges that parents of typical children never experience.

These parents need their church family to offer unconditional love; nonjudgmental hearts; and simple, practical support. Whether it's offering regular prayer support, providing respite care or meals, running errands, providing transportation, or cleaning house, it all makes a difference. When these things happen, children and families thrive, churches function in true community, and the world sees a beautiful picture of the gospel through the flourishing reality of adoption.

Through my work, I've also had the blessing of sharing our family's adoption story both inside Focus and at venues across the country. After sharing at an internal Focus on the Family devotional, Focus's Director of Book Development, Larry Weeden, mentioned that I should write a book.

I was quite flattered but not interested. At that time, we hadn't yet told our kids some of what is in this book. I declined politely, but the idea just wouldn't leave my mind. Eventually, it occurred to me that my inability to let the idea drop might be God's leading.

If John and I were going to write a book, we would need to talk to the kids and get their permission. They'd have to know what they didn't already know. In a stunning series of conversations initiated by the kids over many months, they made it clear that if our family's story would help other kids and families, they were okay with it. In fact, they urged us to do it. Throughout the writing of the book, God provided opportunities to reveal one new detail after another to our kids.

In one pivotal conversation, I asked Daniel if he was sure it was okay for me to talk about the sad choices his birth parents made that hurt him.

"Why would I care if you told that?" my eleven-year-old son said, truly puzzled. "That's not about me; it's about them." He was rather emphatic.

It hit John and me like a ton of bricks that Daniel has an incredibly healthy attitude. His identity isn't wrapped up in the actions of his birth parents, in spite of the fact that those actions caused Daniel to suffer with fetal-alcohol syndrome and Tourette's syndrome. No, he is a child of the King of the Kings and part of Team Rosati.

Through adoption, John and I and our kids experience the stuff of family life together, just like all other families. John and I get to hold our children when they're hurt, laugh together at the funny things of life, stare at our kids' angelic faces when they sleep, rejoice in the normal milestones of life, and teach Daniel, Anna, Joshua, and Hope to walk with the One who makes life worth living. What an incredible honor!

For all of our kids, and indeed for all of us who are believers, our present circumstances and futures aren't defined by our pasts. Our identities are found in Christ alone. As believers in Christ, we were adopted into God's family.

Adoption.

It's a beautiful thing.

Resources

Books

Daly, Jim. *Finding Home: An Imperfect Path to Faith and Family.*
Colorado Springs: David C. Cook, 2007.

Davis, Tom. *Fields of the Fatherless: Discover the Joy of Compassionate Living.* Colorado Springs: David C. Cook, 2008.

Focus on the Family. *Wrapping around Adoptive Families.* Booklet. Colorado Springs: Focus on the Family, 2008.

Mitchell, R. B. *Castaway Kid: One Man's Search for Hope and Home.* Carol Stream, IL: Tyndale, 2007.

Moore, Russell D. *Adopted for Life: The Priority of Adoption for Christian Families and Churches.* Wheaton, IL: Crossway Books, 2009.

Purvis, Karyn B., David R. Cross, and Wendy Lyons Sunshine. *The Connected Child.* New York: McGraw-Hill, 2007.

Sanford, David, and Renée S. Sanford. *Handbook on Thriving as an Adoptive Family: Real-Life Solutions to Common Challenges.* Carol Stream, IL: Tyndale, 2008.

Schooler, Jayne E., and Thomas C. Atwood. *The Whole Life Adoption Book: Realistic Advice for Building a Healthy Adoptive Family.* Colorado Springs: NavPress, 2008.

Weber, Jason. *Launching an Orphans Ministry in Your Church.* Little Rock: FamilyLife Publishing, 2009.

Websites

Cry of the Orphan—www.CryoftheOrphan.org
Empowered to Connect—http://EmpoweredtoConnect.org
I Care About Orphans—www.iCareAboutOrphans.org

The Institute of Child Development, Texas Christian University—
www.Child.TCU.edu

Ministries

Hope for Orphans (www.HopeforOrphans.org)—serves churches
with a heart for orphans in three ways: (1) Mobilizes
and educates Christians about God's heart for orphans,
encouraging them to practice true religion (James 1:27); (2)
Equips lay leaders by providing simple, practical, biblically
based resources to help them launch and sustain orphan
ministries; and (3) Connects key organizations with local
churches by building relationships.

Show Hope (www.ShowHope.org)—a ministry that enables
individuals and communities to change the world for orphans
by not only addressing a child's need for food, shelter, care, and
spiritual nourishment, but also by addressing the root issue for
an orphan: the lack of a family.

Christian Alliance for Orphans (www.ChristianAlliancefor
Orphans.org)—unites more than eighty respected Christian
organizations and a national network of churches in joint
initiatives to inspire, equip, and connect Christians to "defend
the cause of the fatherless" (Isaiah 1:17).

To speak with a trained staff member or counselor at Focus on the
Family, call 800-A-FAMILY (232-6459).

FOCUS ON THE FAMILY®

Welcome to the Family

Whether you purchased this book, borrowed it, or received it as a gift, thanks for reading it! This is just one of many insightful, biblically based resources that Focus on the Family produces for people in all stages of life.

Focus is a global Christian ministry dedicated to helping families thrive as they celebrate and cultivate God's design for marriage and experience the adventure of parenthood. Our outreach exists to support individuals and families in the joys and challenges they face, and to equip and empower them to be the best they can be.

Through our many media outlets, we offer help and hope, promote moral values and share the life-changing message of Jesus Christ with people around the world.

Focus on the Family
MAGAZINES

These faith-building, character-developing publications address the interests, issues, concerns, and challenges faced by every member of your family from preschool through the senior years.

For More
INFORMATION

ONLINE:
Log on to
FocusOnTheFamily.com
In Canada, log on to
FocusOnTheFamily.ca

PHONE:
Call toll-free:
800-A-FAMILY
(232-6459)
In Canada, call toll-free:
800-661-9800

THRIVING FAMILY®	FOCUS ON	FOCUS ON	FOCUS ON
Marriage & Parenting	THE FAMILY	THE FAMILY	THE FAMILY
	CLUBHOUSE JR.®	CLUBHOUSE®	CITIZEN®
	Ages 4 to 8	Ages 8 to 12	U.S. news issues

Rev. 3/11

More Great Resources
from Focus on the Family®

Handbook on Thriving as an Adoptive Family
Real-Life Solutions to Common Challenges
by David and Renée Sanford
Packed with practical advice and ideas for families, this comprehensive handbook addresses the special challenges of parenting adopted children from birth through adulthood and provides real-life solutions.

Small Town, Big Miracle
How Love Came to the Least of These
by W.C. Martin
One church, 72 children. This heart-affirming book tells the tale of the families of Bennett Chapel who adopted 72 of the toughest kids in the foster care system and changed their lives forever. This is a story of the power of redemption and a love that will move and inspire you.

Castaway Kid
One Man's Search for Hope and Home
by R.B. Mitchell
Castaway Kid is the true story of Rob Mitchell, an orphan whose life took a dramatic turn toward a future more promising than he ever imagined. Abandoned by his family when he was just a boy, Rob spent many years feeling angry, rejected, and alone. See how God can transform life's most discouraging circumstances into the adventure of a lifetime.

FOR MORE INFORMATION

Online:
Log on to FocusOnTheFamily.com
In Canada, log on to FocusOnTheFamily.ca

Phone:
Call toll-free: 800-A-FAMILY
In Canada, call toll-free: 800-661-9800

FOCUS
ON THE FAMILY®